MOON

MAYA 2012

A Guide to Celebrations in Mexico, Guatemala, Belize & Honduras

JOSHUA BERMAN

Contents

Discover Maya 2012

December 21, 2012.

This is the date Mesoamerican astronomers calculated and chiseled into stone more than 1,000 years ago based on their observations of the sun, moon, planets, and stars. The Maya considered these celestial objects no less than gods, whose cyclic movements across the sky controlled the passage of time itself.

December 21, 2012, marks the end of the Maya Long Count, a 5,125-year cycle of time that began on August 11, 3114 B.C. Will the cycle repeat? Will the Long Count click over (peacefully or otherwise) to begin a new era for all of humanity? What were the Maya trying to tell us across the millennia?

Whatever the answer to such unanswerable questions, one thing is certain: 2012 presents a once-in-a-lifetime travel opportunity. The Mundo Maya – Mexico, Guatemala, Belize, and Honduras – is where most of the world's 10 million Maya reside today, and the opportunity for interesting and immersive tourism in 2012 is enormous.

Despite what you may have heard, there is little evidence of a Maya prophecy connecting 2012 to any foreseen event, whether cataclysmic or transcendent. Still, the end of such a large cycle – 13 *b'aktuns* of 393

years each – is important, and the date is significant enough that each country in the Mundo Maya is planning a yearlong uplifting of Maya culture, from government-sponsored celebrations to village homestays and grassroots eco-tourism.

This book offers a glimpse of what's planned and where to go. Expect special Maya-themed tours, events, ceremonies, symposiums, and celebrations at both minor and major archaeological sites. Watch the summer solstice sunrise from the Canaa pyramid at Caracol in Belize. Decipher the famed Long Count inscription on Stela I at Cobá in Mexico. Celebrate equinox in the Guatemala forest with Maya elders at Uaxactún. Sweat out some toxins in a Maya *temazcal*, a ritual steam bath, near Copán, Honduras. Share a meal of corn tortillas and beans with a Maya family – and ask what *they* think about the Maya calendar and 2012.

Welcome to the New Era. Let's get started.

Planning Your Trip

▶ WHERE TO GO

To see as many deep-jungle temples and pyramids as possible, pick a corner of the Mundo Maya with both a high density and wide variety of archaeological sites. You'll also want to be near modern Maya villages and natural attractions like waterfalls, cenotes, beaches, caves, and volcanoes. Luckily there are plenty of places that meet all these criteria and more.

Mexico

The number of Maya sites in Mexico dwarfs the rest of the Maya countries. Mexico has massive, accessible archaeological sites like Chichén Itzá, Uxmal, and Cobá; it also has alluring, hard-to-reach ruins such as Yaxchilán, accessible only by *lancha* up the Usumacinta River. Mexico also has the largest number of archaeological sites with direct relevance to the Long Count and 2012, including Izapa, considered "ground zero" for the Long Count.

Guatemala

Guatemala has the most living Maya communities, most of the world's Maya population, and the most surviving spoken Mayan languages. Guatemala is the true heartland of the Maya, home to more than six million people of various lineages speaking dozens of languages. This is also where the old

jaguar mask on a temple at Lamanai

Chichén Itzà's thousand-year-old brick walls hide many secrets.

way of life and sacred calendars are kept, especially in the Cuchumatan Mountains. Guatemala's archaeological sites are big ones: Tikal, Uaxactún, Quiriguá, Yaxhá, and Piedras Negras. Its large concentration of Maya communities and sites with Long Count significance make it a natural base for 2012.

Belize

Belize is a small English-speaking, relaxed, and fascinating country. Its 320,000 inhabitants speak eight different languages and are spread over an area the size of Massachusetts. Belize has some of the most expansive, wild-life-filled tropical forests in the world, an enormous cave system packed with Maya artifacts, and Classic Maya Period cities like Lamanai, still mostly forested, and Caracol, over the Mountain Pine Ridge. Belize also has diving along the hemisphere's longest barrier reef.

Though living Maya make up only about 10 percent of the population, Belize was once home to many more and is riddled with archaeological sites. San Ignacio, in western Belize, allows access to the main sites as well as a range of jungle lodges. A community tourism program in the southern Toledo District allows travelers a chance to spend a few nights in a rural Maya village.

Honduras

Copán was declared a UNESCO World Heritage Site in 1980 and continues to be one of the most undervalued destinations in Central America. This unique city by the Copán River in western Honduras was a major population and cultural center during the height of the Classic Period, from the 5th to 9th centuries A.D. It is famous for its intricate writings and layers of kingdoms built one on top of the other. A lush landscape of river valleys and hills surrounds the ruins. Copán makes an excellent, offbeat alternative on the 2012 path. It is a powerful spot, but won't attract the crowds expected in Mexico.

▶ WHEN TO GO

High season in the Mundo Maya falls mid-December through May, often with sunny skies and green vegetation during the North American winter. However, November can be dry as a bone and sunny, while December, January, and even February can play host to wet "cold fronts" that sometimes sit around for days.

June, July, and August technically form the rainy season in the Mundo Maya. This could mean everything from a quick afternoon shower to days of rain. This green season is a beautiful, if humid, time to visit. Accommodations are often discounted significantly during this period. August is most popular with European travelers, while December and February are dominated by North Americans. Some businesses shut down completely during the months of September and October, the peak of hurricane season.

Important Events

The most well-known event in 2012 is, of course, December 21, but there will be events and ceremonies on each solstice and equinox date at different sites throughout the Mundo Maya. Plan your trip around one of these dates if you're curious how they may be observed:

- Spring equinox: March 20
- Summer solstice: June 20
- Fall equinox: September 22
- Winter solstice: December 21
- The winter solstice also happens to fall in the middle of the peak holiday season in most tourist areas. Accommodations near major Maya sites may be fully booked in advance—and rates may increase closer to the date.

owl dancer at Xcaret on the Riviera Maya

Actun Tunichil Muknal's Crystal Maiden, Belize

▶ BEFORE YOU GO

Do some homework on Maya history and the Maya calendar—the depth and complexity of the 2012 story is surprising. For more practical details and strategies within each country, consult the travel planners on www.moon.com.

Passports and Visas

Good news for multi-country Mundo Maya tourists: In June 2006, Guatemala, El Salvador, Honduras, and Nicaragua entered the "Central America-4 Border Control Agreement" (CA-4); citizens of the four countries may travel freely across land borders between these countries without completing entry and exit formalities at immigration checkpoints. U.S. citizens may travel among these four countries without visas or tourist entry permits. You'll still need a passport, but it will be easier to hop around in the Mundo Maya.

When entering Belize, U.S. citizens will receive a 30-day automatic tourist card. Entering Mexico by air, U.S. citizens will need a passport and must pay a small fee to obtain a tourist card (also known as an FMM and often included in cost of your plane ticket).

Before any trip, check online (http://travel.state.gov) for the latest entry and exit requirements for each country.

Vaccinations

Many cities in the United States and Canada have medical travel clinics that can advise on the latest recommended and required vaccinations on a country-by-country basis.

The U.S. Centers for Disease Control and Prevention (CDC) has a Traveler Health webpage (wwwnc.cdc.gov/travel). It recommends routine vaccinations (chickenpox/varicella, polio, MMR, DPT) be updated to protect travelers from diseases prevalent in other countries.

As of late 2011, the CDC reports that areas in Mexico with malaria include Chiapas and rural areas in the states of Nayarit, Oaxaca, and Sinaloa, with rare cases in Quintana Roo and Tabasco. In Guatemala, malaria has been reported only in rural areas lower than 1,500 meters above sea level. In Belize, malaria has been reported in all areas except Belize City and islands popular with tourists.

If traveling to a country for an extended time, check the CDC's recommendations for vaccine-preventable diseases (hepatitis A and B, typhoid, and rabies), which vary by country and situation.

Travel Hubs

Mexico is the easiest and cheapest country to reach from the U.S. or Canada, with a steady schedule of direct flights to Cancún, Mérida, and Villahermosa. Most current security concerns are in the north, a thousand miles from the Maya area. The cheapest flights to the Mundo Maya are frequently to large Mexico hubs such as Cancún.

Mérida is a comfortable colonial base from which to explore the Yucatán. Its international airport is serviced by airlines within the U.S. and Mexico.

Due to consistently expensive fares to Belize City, travelers sometimes use Cancún as a more affordable way to get to Belize (but it requires a six-hour bus ride to the border at Chetumal, Mexico). From Chetumal, you can also easily cross into northern Belize and Corozal Town, with access to several notable Maya archeological sites.

Guatemala City makes a perfect base not only for travel within Guatemala, but throughout the Mundo Maya. Travelers can begin in Guatemala City and make side trips to Honduras, Belize, and remote Izapa in Mexico.

Explore Maya 2012

Exploring Mesoamerica's Mundo Maya includes the Maya archaeological sites and people in Mexico's Yucatán peninsula, Campeche, and Chiapas; all of Guatemala and Belize; Honduras's Copán, and a few places in El Salvador. In 2012, with the world's attention pointed their way, these countries are safer, more established, and more accessible destinations than ever before. Each will celebrate the end of the Long Count in their own way.

To travel through the Mundo Maya, combine trips to archaeological sites with visits to living Maya villages. Travel independently, sign up for a tour with a Maya calendar or "Sacred Maya Journey" theme, visit an active archaeological dig, spend the night with a modern Maya family, travel by helicopter to an ancient city, or race in La Ruta Maya River Challenge. Whatever you choose to do in 2012, book it *now*. At press time, rooms were already filling up for the week of the winter solstice in 2012.

▶ THE BEST ARCHAEOLOGICAL SITES TO VISIT IN 2012

Temples, observatories, plazas, and ball courts will fill your days as you visit the main sites of the Maya world. Most structures you'll see were built well over 1,000 years ago and were subsequently abandoned around A.D. 900. Many of these lost cities have been fully excavated while others are half-covered by abundant growth and wildlife. Archaeological breakthroughs happen frequently, especially as new technology reveals more of the forest floor and what lies beneath it.

Many sites have a visitors center and, sometimes, a museum or interpretive display near the entrance. Both freelance and official tour guides are often available. True Maya calendar/archaeology buffs will want to target the following specific sites.

Mexico

Equinox dates (spring, Mar. 20; fall, Sept. 22) are huge events at many sites, but are especially impressive at Chichén Itzá. This is the day the sun casts a shadow on the El Castillo

Temple of the Frescoes, Cobá

temple, projecting an image of a snake descending the stairs.

Among the uncrowded ruins at Cobá is the very long date on Stela 1 in the Macanxoc Group.

Palenque has several Long Count date glyphs, both past and future, including a count indicating there are 20, not 13, *b'aktuns* in the

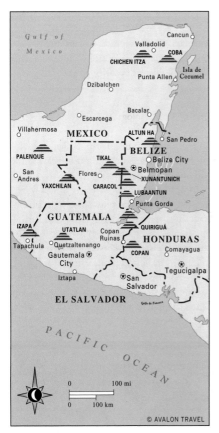

6, contains the only text in the Maya world bearing the actual date of December 21, 2012. Monument 6 is now housed in a museum in Villahermosa, Mexico.

Guatemala

The date on Stela 29 at Tikal bears an early Long Count. In addition to major winter solstice events, Tikal will host a ceremony and celebrations for the Día de La Raza (Day of the Races) on October 21, 2012.

Spring (Mar. 20) and fall (Sept. 22) equinoxes are a big deal at Uaxactún. A host of special ceremonies are planned for 2012. Join in sunrise ceremonies and vigils at an ancient observatory and watch a reenactment of the ancient Maya ball game.

At Quiriguá, Stelae E and A have 3114 B.C. texts on 10.5-meter-tall (35-foot-tall) statues. Zenith passages at this latitude occur on May 1 and November 11.

Belize

On February 18, Altun Ha hosts the Maya Fest (including the Kinich Ahau Art Exhibition) with local crafts, food and drink, entertainment, and exhibits.

Xunantunich will be the site of the country's biggest event on December 21, 2012. December 22–23 will see a Fire Ceremony and Gala, an overnight event to bring in the New Age. Visitors can watch a Youth Torch Run from other Maya temples to Xunantunich.

Catch the sunrise over the E Group in Plaza A at Caracol during spring equinox (Mar. 20) and summer solstice (June 20).

On December 21, head south to the ruins of Lubaantun for a smaller, more exclusive celebration and concert.

Honduras

Copán bears a mention of the 9th *b'aktun* ending and multiple references to 3114 B.C. (the beginning of the Long Count). Lying at the same

cycle. If you visit during summer solstice, you may witness the dawn hierophany, or "trick of light and shadow," in the Temple of the Sun.

Yaxchilán has a Long Count date with cycles above the 13 *b'aktun,* all with the co-efficient 13. Look for them on the ball-game panels under Temple 33.

Izapa has several fine examples of creation myth imagery, and the alignment of its structures may suggest that ancient Izapans were projecting forward to illustrate the 2012 night sky.

Tortuguero no longer exists as an archaeological site (it now lies beneath a cement factory), but its most famous relic, Monument

latitude as Izapa to the west, Copán has similar dark rift and galactic alignment imagery on some of its monuments. Copán's zenith passage dates are May 1 and August 12. Nadir passages are February 13 and October 31.

The week of the winter solstice promises the Maya Festival Copán. Archaeological seminars, a fire ceremony, mass meditation, musical presentations, and children's activities highlight this event.

▶ THE LONG COUNT

Of the known Maya archaeological sites in the Maya world, only a handful give direct clues as to the Long Count ending in 2012. Of these, only a single stela bears the actual date December 21, 2012 (or 13 *b'aktun,* or 13.0.0.0.0). It is written on a damaged stone slab called Tortuguero Monument 6, which resides in a museum basement in Villahermosa, Mexico, off-limits to the public.

There are dozens of inscriptions you can seek out that refer to the Long Count start date of 3114 B.C. and scores more that suggest the importance of the endings of large cycles (*k'atuns* and *b'aktuns*), perhaps providing clues as to what the Maya foresaw at the end of 13 *b'aktuns.*

In addition to messages in hieroglyphics and writing, the physical orientation of structures at archaeological sites (e.g., lining up temples and statues to the solstice sunrise and other celestial events) can have relevance to 2012. The best example is found at Izapa, where building orientation and inscribed imagery both may point directly to what the Maya calculated would appear in the night sky in December 2012.

The figure in the middle of this Maya calendar is the bearer of time.

▶ SPECIALTY TOURS AND PACKAGES IN 2012

Throughout 2012, every country in the Maya world will host events and ceremonies at most of the ancient sites. The majority of 2012 activities will be celebrations of Maya culture, both ancient and modern. Most tours are anchored with visits to relevant archaeological sites, to Maya villages, consults with astrologers, and lectures from archaeologists and epigraphers.

Another way to acknowledge 2012 is to help out in a rural Maya community, either by donating to a foundation that helps the modern Maya, or by participating in a homestay or simple tourism program.

A handful of community-based tourism opportunities exist throughout the region, some quite primitive and authentic. Your support of these programs in 2012 and beyond helps allow modern Maya to diversify their income.

Mexico

Ancient Maya Calendars and Astronomy: Spring Equinox 2012 Tour: Combines tours to Chichén Itzá, Dzibilchaltun, Uxmal, Tulum, Cobá, and Ek Balam with lectures about the Maya calendar and ancient astronomy. Stand beneath Chichén Itzá's Castillo Pyramid as the shadow snake descends on the spring equinox.

El Hombre Sobre La Tierra: Join this established eco-tourism project in the Maya village of Muchucuxcah where you can spend your nights in hammocks, eat local meals, and learn a Maya trade such as weaving or *palapa* construction.

Maya Calendar and Glyph Workshop: Learn the fundamentals of Maya writing and the Maya calendar, then test your knowledge in the field at archaeological sites like Palenque, Bonampak, Yaxchilán, and Tonina.

Mayan Sacred Journey: Xcaret Ecopark will reenact a Maya crossing to Cozumel with 300 canoe paddlers dressed in ancient Maya clothing, ornaments, and body paint.

Traveling in Maya Time 2012 Solstice

Chichén Itzá will host major solstice and equinox events in 2012.

the Mayan Sacred Journey, reenacted at Xcaret

Trips: Celebrates the beginning of a new era with visits to Cobá, Ek Balam, Chichén Itzá, cenotes, and the colonial cities of Valladolid and Mérida.

2012, A New K'atun Begins: Three tours, led by a Maya spiritual leader, focus on enlightenment and self-discovery in 2012.

Yaxunah Centro Cultural: Volunteers are invited to share their knowledge and experience with this indigenous community.

Guatemala

Birthplace of the Maya Long Count Calendar: This tour of Maya culture through the ages visits archaeological sites with the earliest Long Count calendar dates, as well as stunning Maya lake villages. Includes: Tak'alik Ab'aj, Ixmiche, Santiago de Atitlán, Chichicastenango, Quetzaltenango, Antigua, and Izapa.

Dawn of a New Age: Activities are based at beautiful Lake Atitlán and include Maya cuisine, a fire ceremony, Maya spiritual cleansings, and a reading of your Maya birth date.

Guatemala, A Sacred Land–2012: Get deep into the Mundo Maya, including homestays in nearby Cakchiquel and Tz'utujil Maya villages.

Huehuetenango Community Ecological Tourism Project: Huehuetenango is ground zero for grassroots, village-based eco-tourism. These projects are the first of their kind and are visited by just a handful of visitors.

7 Sacred Mayan Fire Ceremonies in 7 Sacred Sites Over 7 Days: Learn your Maya birth glyph, participate in ceremonies, visit archaeological sites, sample local food and drink, and learn about Maya cosmology.

Belize

Archaeology Tour plus Tikal: Attend lectures on the Maya calendar and the possibility of a new cycle, then visit Lamanai, Xunantunich, Caracol, and Cahal Pech,

the view from El Castillo, Xunantunich, the site of Belize's biggest winter solstice celebration in 2012

before spending the night under the stars at Tikal (just across the border in Guatemala).

Belize It 2012: This weeklong tour includes a trip to Actun Tunichil Muknal cave and a private full-day tour of Lamanai.

La Ruta Maya River Challenge: This is Belize's Super Bowl, an exciting and convivial canoe race held during the first week of March and timed to coincide with Baron Bliss Day celebrations.

Maya Winter Solstice 2012: The Lodge at Chaa Creek offers an expansive 2012 winter solstice program. On December 22, a huge stela will be erected, inscribed with the names of participating guests.

Toledo Ecotourism Association: This eco-tourism program organizes homestays in Maya villages. Activities include craft lessons, storytelling, and tours.

Year of the Maya: Many jungle resort packages in 2012 include tours to Xunantunich, Caracol, and Cahal Pech, morning forest walks, visits to sacred caves such as Actun Tunichil Muknal, and sometimes a side trip to Tikal.

Honduras

Temazcal: After a full day touring the Copán ruins, sign up for this Maya ritual sweat bath. The Copán Valley boasts several yoga retreats and forest-bound boutique spas.

▶ THE MAYA OF TODAY

As Rigoberta Menchú reminded the world in 1992 upon accepting the Nobel Peace Prize, "We are not myths of the past, ruins in the jungle or zoos. We are people and we want to be respected, not to be victims of intolerance and racism."

Today there are as many as 10 million Maya living in their ancestral lands and abroad. In some areas, the rural population lives much as they have for many centuries; their daykeepers, or spiritual guides, continue to maintain ancient Maya calendars. Elsewhere, the Maya are as modern as anyone else in the world.

"The Maya" are actually an extremely diverse group, and clumping them together under

purification ceremony at Lubaantun, Belize

the label "modern" or "living" is problematic. They speak some 30 Mayan languages and, as a whole, make up one of the largest intact indigenous populations in the world.

Many Maya are proud of their shared heritage, and have begun a kind of cultural renaissance in the 21st century. In the year 2012, look for workshops in Maya cosmology, medicine, weaving, and language — especially in hubs like Mérida, San Cristóbal de las Casas, Flores, and Antigua. There are also community-based tourism projects in Maya villages throughout the region.

Some people see the age of 2012 as a time for our various cultures to share their wisdom in a way that will benefit all. In his book *The Living Maya,* Dr. Robert Sitler discusses some of the more admirable values maintained by the Maya, which we non-Maya could benefit from: "Cherish our babies, connect with our communities, revere the natural world that sustains us, seek the wisdom of humanity's elders, and immerse ourselves in direct experience of this divine world."

The way forward in 2012, he says, is to embrace these living values of the Maya.

MEXICO

There is an art to sleeping in a hammock. I learned this after a week of research in the Yucatán Maya village of Muchucuxcah. I'm talking about how to get a healthy night's sleep while strung between two poles in a thatch-roof *palapa,* the way the Maya have been sleeping in their homes for thousands of years. Our homemade hammocks, made right in the village, were comfortable, but it was tricky to get situated. I had to lie diagonally, across the axis where it hangs, in order to straighten out enough to rest. And I still woke often to the geckos chirping or for a night hike to the latrine.

But each night got a little easier, and every morning for a week our "solidarity tourism" group would rise and emerge from our huts, achy-backed and sleep-crusted. The huts were positioned in a loose circle around a water tower and a shared bathroom. They were constructed with the help of visiting groups, like ours, who wanted to volunteer in a Maya village while at the same time meeting community members and learning something about their lives.

I was guiding a multigenerational Seattle delegation of American Jewish World Service volunteers, and we helped build the last few structures. It was fascinating work; we prepared and assembled the materials using traditional Maya methods and tools.

In the morning, we splashed water on our faces at the central *pila* then soaked in the birdsong as we joined our assigned families for breakfast. There, in homes with carefully swept dirt floors and traditional kitchen hearths, excited

© JOSHUA BERMAN

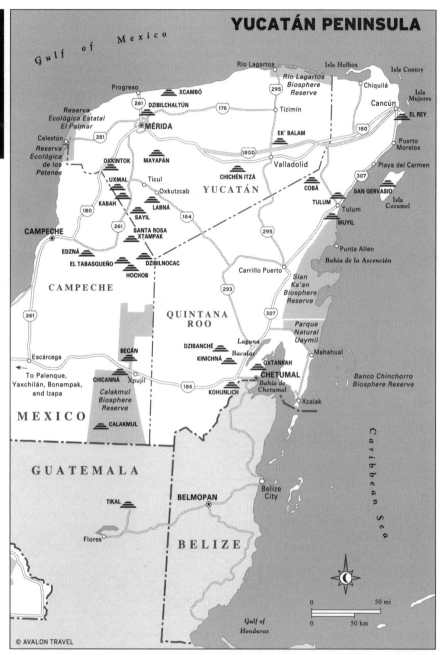

YUCATÁN PENINSULA

© AVALON TRAVEL

children and animals greeted us as we sat down to a table full of eggs, beans, country cheese, and *comal*-toasted tortillas. Our days were full of sweat and dirt, meetings and talks, activities and interactions—both in Muchucuxcah and on day trips to Chichén Itzá and nearby towns. This was my introduction to Mexico's Mundo Maya, and I still have much to explore.

HISTORY

The Yucatán peninsula was settled primarily according to the location of fresh water sources, since it is mostly flat, low, and without rivers. That's why so many Maya archaeological sites and modern communities are built near swamps and cenotes. By about 1000 B.C., farming villages in what is now the states of Veracruz and Tabasco had begun developing the Olmec culture. They created a Long Count calendar and hieroglyphic writing system, which were crucial contributions to the Maya society. The Olmec extended their influence south, into the Preclassic Maya empire of Izapa. The Izapans made important advances in the use of various calendar systems, including the Long Count. Other strong Preclassic city-states like Tikal and El Mirador pushed north from Guatemala's Petén into the Yucatán, whose ascending cities had received the Long Count by the end of the third century A.D. Thus began more than a millennium of shifting power and alliances throughout the Mexican Mundo Maya, ending in its near total collapse in A.D. 900.

Of the surviving Mexican Maya, their knowledge of ancient systems, including the Long Count, migrated south or disappeared (until Western explorers dug them up centuries later). After the cities were abandoned, illiterate, warring cultures—including Toltecs from the north and Itzá from the west—stepped in. The Itzá established short-lived dynasties across Mexico's Mundo Maya, with Chichén Itzá ruling all. Chichén finally fell in A.D. 1224, and the scattered indigenous peoples of the Yucatán repeated the cycles of war, peace, and migration, all the way up to and through the Spanish conquest in the 1500s.

Ever since the first garrison Cortés sent up the Grijalva River in Chiapas was beaten back by fierce Maya, the people of this area have had a reputation for resistance. It took many years and several Maya uprisings before the colonizers finally gained control over Chiapas and set it up to produce cash crops for export (sugar, cattle, coffee, timber), which meant forcing rural Maya to gather in villages and converting them to Christianity.

Tension between indigenous, Spanish, and Ladino erupted in the Caste Wars, a period of hundreds of years of violence throughout the Yucatán marked by violent revenge cycles between the different races and classes. Quintana Roo, adjacent to Belize along the Caribbean Coast, was a no-man's-land for more than a hundred years.

The 20th century saw the Mexican revolution and significant land distribution and subsidies for indigenous farmers, but in the 1990s, all of that was undone when President Carlos Salinas de Gortari removed the constitutional provision guaranteeing land for all farmers; he also privatized the collective peasant organizations that had existed for most of the century. The North American Free Trade Agreement was passed around this time, further disempowering Mexico's small-scale Maya farmers and acting as catalyst for the rise of the Zapatista revolutionary movement, a leftist organization based in Chiapas, where about one third of the population is Maya. One of the Zapatistas' main demands is increased power, land, and respect for the indigenous people of Mexico and the world.

Today, you'll find Yucatec Maya culture and language dominant throughout the Yucatán, Quintana Roo, and into Belize, while the Chiapas highlands are occupied by Tzeltal- and Tzotzil-speaking Maya, with pockets of Lakandon, Tojolabal, Chol, and Chontal.

ORIENTATION

The Yucatán peninsula is a 70,000-square-mile flat shelf of limestone surrounded on three sides by the Caribbean Sea, comprising the large Mexican states of Yucatán, Campeche, and Quintana Roo. The Maya area here continues south and southwest, along the border

MEXICO

© JOSHUA BERMAN

the great ball court at Chichén Itzá

with Guatemala's vast Petén wilderness and into the Chiapas highlands.

PLANNING YOUR TIME

The principal Maya sites in the Yucatán are **Chichén Itzá, Uxmal, Cobá,** and Tulum. In addition to the tourist scene on the coast (Cancún, Riviera Maya, Playa del Carmen), there are several noteworthy community tourism programs near Chichén Itzá where you can stay in a Maya village and swim in cenotes. (Though Tulum's archaelogical site is heavily touristed, it has little significance to 2012 and the Long Count. For more information, consult *Moon Cancún & Cozumel.*)

Mexico's Mundo Maya is vast. Far and away, **Cancún** has the most popular and economical airport for this region. **Cancún International** (CUN, www.cancun-airport.com) receives direct international flights daily.

From Cancún, it's a four-hour bus ride, or a short connecting flight, to **Mérida.** Mérida is hands-down the best option for serious Mayaphiles who also enjoy pampering. You'll have immediate access to Uxmal archaeological site and the Puuc Route, plus a fine selection of accommodations, daily music and dance performances, classes, museums, and remarkable architecture. Many Maya-themed workshops, events, and celebrations will be centered in Mérida. Uxmal, the area's premier Terminal Classic Maya archaeological site, is only one hour to the south, on the road to Campeche.

The state of **Campeche** is up-and-coming, an undervalued and spectacular part of Mexico's Mundo Maya. Most notable are the ruins in the Río Bec region in southern Campeche, including Calakmul, with the largest known Maya pyramid. Campeche City itself has excellent museums and nearby ruins.

Villahermosa provides access to Palenque and San Cristóbal de las Casas. Devote at least four days to Palenque, one of the finest archaeological sites in the world. Afterwards, book a *lancha* upriver to Yaxchilán and Bonampak, sites that still feel like lost cities in the forest.

San Cristóbal de las Casas, the main base for exploring the state of Chiapas, is less popular among North American visitors, but a major destination for Europeans. There are fewer impressive archaeological sites in this region; a base here is more about excursions into the Chiapas highlands.

Die-hards will continue to the city of **Tapachula** and the nearby archaeological site of Izapa, near the Pacific Coast and the border with Guatemala. Izapa was the seat of a once-mighty Preclassic empire and, based on the evidence, the possible birthplace of the Long Count calendar cycle. Combine a visit here with an incursion into Guatemala, whose highland Maya sites are just over yonder.

In 2012

Mexico has some of the most relevant sites to 2012 and the Long Count in all of the Mundo Maya, starting with **Izapa** on the southwest Pacific Coast, where the Long Count is believed to have originated. Near **Villahermosa**, Tortuguero (a site that now lies beneath a cement factory) produced the only known inscription of the actual date December 21, 2012, yet found. There are also myriad interesting Long Count and "deep time" dates at sites like **Cobá** and **Yaxchilán.**

Maya Archaeological Sites

Mexico has every kind of site from every era of the Maya and beyond: from grand cities to humble sacred spots; from Preclassic to Terminal Classic; from easily accessed to difficult-to-reach destinations. All archaeological sites are managed by **El Instituto Nacional de Antropología e Historia** (INAH, tel. 4040-4624 and 4040-4300, www.inah.gob.mx). INAH reports that there are 29,000 registered archaeological sites in all of Mexico, of which 180 are open to the public. A good many of those are in the Maya zone.

There are increasingly more restrictions about climbing the pyramids. All are site specific and are enforced both for your safety and the park guards' sanity. For example, at Palenque, the Temple of Inscriptions and the Temple of the Jaguar are closed to climbers, but the Cross Group and the Palace are still open. At Chichén Itzá, forget about climbing anything. As a rule, if you see a "no climbing" sign, abide by it. If you don't see a sign, be careful—especially in the rain and early-morning mist when the limestone gets very slick.

CHICHÉN ITZÁ

Chichén Itzá is the lordly rock star of the Mundo Maya. A UNESCO World Heritage Site since 1988, it is one of the New Seven Wonders of the World and an inspirational backdrop for performances by artists such as Elton John and Luciano Pavarotti.

This grand capital of the Yucatán may have been home to as many as 50,000 Maya during its heyday in the Late Classic and Postclassic periods. After Chichén's Maya population collapsed around A.D. 900, an invasion of northern Nahuatl-speaking Toltecs were followed by the Itzá, all of whom continued to build on the site. What is left is a stunning smorgasbord of Mesoamerican culture and architecture spread across a massive complex of temples, palaces, altars, and the largest ball court in the Maya world.

The Ruins

Some of the most important structures (the ball court and Temple of Kukulcán) were erected toward the end of the Maya rule, possibly triggered by an auspicious calendar cycle ending in A.D. 830. **El Castillo** (Temple of Kukulcán) is an iconic stepped pyramid 24 meters (79 feet) tall and dating to around A.D. 850. This structure is famous for having various Maya calendar cycles represented in the number of steps, platforms, sides, and levels, all of which are aligned with the equinox sun, such that on those days only (and for a few days before and after the equinox dates), a serpent-shaped shadow descends the steps.

Chichén has the greatest **ball court** in the Mundo Maya (the field stretches 135 meters, or 443 feet). The level field between flat walls soars eight meters (26 feet), broken only by the

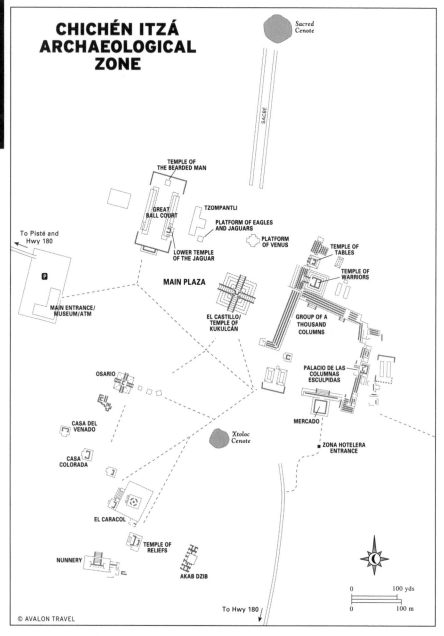

CHICHÉN ITZÁ ARCHAEOLOGICAL ZONE

Sacred Cenote

SACBÉ

TEMPLE OF THE BEARDED MAN

GREAT BALL COURT

TZOMPANTLI

PLATFORM OF EAGLES AND JAGUARS

PLATFORM OF VENUS

LOWER TEMPLE OF THE JAGUAR

To Pisté and Hwy 180

MAIN PLAZA

TEMPLE OF TABLES

TEMPLE OF WARRIORS

P

MAIN ENTRANCE/ MUSEUM/ATM

EL CASTILLO/ TEMPLE OF KUKULCÁN

GROUP OF A THOUSAND COLUMNS

OSARIO

PALACIO DE LAS COLUMNAS ESCULPIDAS

CASA DEL VENADO

MERCADO

CASA COLORADA

Xtoloc Cenote

ZONA HOTELERA ENTRANCE

EL CARACOL

TEMPLE OF RELIEFS

NUNNERY

AKAB DZIB

To Hwy 180

0   100 yds

0   100 m

© AVALON TRAVEL

circular rings through which the hard rubber ball had to pass.

Don't miss the **Tzompantli** (Wall of Skulls), which features rows of staring skull carvings: rows of skulls, skulls on a rack, eagles eating human hearts, and death warriors holding shields. (Photo ops galore, and inspiration for the name of your next death metal band.)

Crucial to the location of the city, the **Sacred Cenote** is a 100-foot-deep natural well, located 300 meters (985 feet) north of the main city at the end of a limestone road. This is where the Maya made many sacrifices, both human and material. The rain gods must have been very hungry: dredging revealed scores of skeletons, many women and children. Archaeologists have also found many precious jade items at the bottom of the water. Watch your step.

Though tourists may not enter the **Temple of Warriors,** they can admire the carvings on its south facade. Human faces emerge from serpents' mouths, and four hook-nosed Chaac masks look on. Next to this building is the photogenic **Group of a Thousand Columns,** the Maya's conceptual answer to China's Terracotta Army.

Rising several stories atop a small hill, **El Caracol** is an especially important structure in Chichén Itzá, named for the spiral staircase that leads to what may have been an astronomical observatory. The site is perfectly aligned with the solstice sun; its window slits align to the path of the moon during the spring equinox.

Visiting the Site

Chichén Itzá is open 8 A.M.–5 P.M. Tuesday through Sunday. Entrance costs US$10 (plus US$3.50 video camera fee). The fee includes entrance to the park and the sound-and-light show, whether you stay for it or not. You'll also be offered the option of a tour guide (US$50–60 per group).

Chichén Itzá is a huge, well-groomed, and micro-managed site with a lot of rules and ropes. At the entrance is an ATM, bag storage, cafeteria, bookstore, and gift shop—and a constant stream of tour buses loading and

unloading in the large parking area. It's usually all quite efficient.

As one of the premier day-trip destinations from Cancún and cruise-ship ports, Chichén Itzá is swarmed by tens of thousands of visitors in the middle of the day. Definitely consider staying at an on-site accommodation to experience the site during the cooler (mellower) mornings or late afternoons. The **Lodge at Chichén Itzá** (tel. 800/235-4079, www.mayaland.com, US$250) has 39 bungalows amid the ruins, and is home to its own private collection of unexcavated ruins. The lodge also has a private entrance to Chichén Itzá, which allows guests to avoid the Disneyland-esque lines at the main entrance.

A quick visit to the **museum** at the visitors center is worth it, and you may as well stay for the **Sound and Light Show** (7 P.M. Oct.–Apr.; 8 P.M. May–Sept.).

In 2012

All **equinox dates** are already huge events at Chichén Itzá, since this is the day that the sun casts a shadow on El Castillo that looks like a snake descending the stairs. Expect a series of large events and gatherings here, probably more in a celebratory mood. (I would not be surprised if there is a reenactment of the ball game, at least on the solstice dates.)

Getting There

Chichén Itzá is located on Highway 180 between **Mérida** (1.5 hours away) and **Cancún** (2.5 hours away). The easiest way to arrange a day trip from Mérida or Cancún is with your hotel or a local tour company.

By car from either Mérida or Cancún, take the *autopista* (US$7 from Mérida, US$22 from Cancún). Exit at the village of Pisté and follow signs to the site.

Chichén Itzá is 1.5 kilometers (1 mi) from the bus station in the small town of Pisté. Buses to and from Pisté stop at both the entrance to Chichén Itzá and the bus station. There are also buses to and from Cancún, Cobá, Mérida, Tulum, and Valladolid. By bus from Mérida, take a first-class ADO bus or one of the first-

CENOTES: SACRED SINKHOLES

Cenotes are limestone sinkholes, sometimes hundreds of meters deep and filled with crystalline freshwater, fed by underground rivers. Cenotes owe their formation to the massive meteorite that hit the Yucatán Peninsula 65 million years ago. The impact shattered the peninsula's thick limestone cap like a stone hitting a car windshield, and in the millions of years that followed, rainwater seeped into the cracks, carving huge underground caverns and hundreds of kilometers of channels out of the highly soluble limestone. Cenotes are former caverns whose roofs collapsed. Together the channels form the world's longest underground river system.

Cenotes were sacred to Maya, who relied on them for water and viewed them as apertures to the underworld. (The name is derived from the Yucatec Maya word dz'onot.) Sacrificial victims were sometimes thrown into their eerie depths, along with finely worked stone and clay items, and archaeologists have learned a great deal about early Maya rituals by dredging cenotes near archaeological sites, most notably Chichén Itzá. Indeed, the name Chichén Itzá means "Well of the Itzá," undoubtedly a reference to the ancient city's dramatic cenote.

Today the peninsula's cenotes attract worshippers of a different sort: snorkelers and scuba divers. The unbelievably clear water – with 100-meter (328-foot) visibility in places – is complimented by what other inland and underground diving environments (like lakes and flooded mines) lack: stunning stalactites and stalagmites. During early ice ages, water drained from the cenotes, giving time for the slow-growing features to form. When the climate warmed, the cenotes filled with water once again, their depths now forested with dramatic stone spires, pillars, and columns.

Divers with open-water certification can dive in the cenotes. Though "full-cave" diving requires advanced training, most cenote tours are actually "cavern" dives, meaning you are always within 40 meters (130 feet) of an air pocket. It's a good idea to take some open-water dives before your first cenote tour – buoyancy control is especially important in cenotes, and you'll be contending with different weights and finning technique.

Many Mexican cenotes are open to the public, and their cool clear water is perfect for swimming, snorkeling, and scuba diving. Visitor facilities range from simple restrooms and snorkel rental to full-service "cenote parks" with guided tours. Some favorites include:

RIVIERA MAYA

Cenote Cristalino: Cristalino has an overhanging cliff, similar to Jardín de Edén next door, but a smaller swimming area.

Jardín de Edén: The best and biggest of a cluster of cenotes near Playa Xpu-Há, with a large cavern that forms a dramatic overhang.

Ruta de los Cenotes: Sure, some spots along the "Cenote Route" are tourist traps, but others are sublime, like Siete Bocas, a huge eerie cavern filled with shimmering water, and Lucerno Verde, a gorgeous open-air pool filled with freshwater turtles and fish.

CHICHÉN ITZÁ

Cenote Ik-Kil: Just three kilometers (1.8 miles) from Chichén Itzá, this huge deep cenote can be crowded, but it is impressive all the same.

---

class buses to Cancún. Otherwise, buy a second-class bus ticket to Valladolid and travel first-class from there.

COBÁ

Cobá means "Water Stirred by Wind." Located in the state of Quintana Roo, Cobá was founded around A.D. 100 close to several freshwater lagoons. If Cobá was not the largest city in all the Mundo Maya, it was at least close. The city sprawled over 35 square miles and had thousands of structures (most still unexcavated) and miles of raised roads (or *sacbeob,* the plural of *saq'be,* which means "white road"), and was home to 50,000 people.

Cobá doesn't have the beach of nearby

© JOSHUA BERMAN

You can swim, snorkel, float, and dive in the cenotes of the Yucatán.

Cenote Yokdzonot: This little-known gem is all the more rewarding for being operated by a cooperative of enterprising local women.

TULUM AND COBÁ
Car Wash: This innocuous-looking cenote, just past Gran Cenote, has stunning rock formations below the surface.

Cenote Choo-Ha: One of four dramatic cenotes near Cobá, with a high domed ceiling and iridescent blue water.

Dos Ojos and **Hidden Worlds:** Side-by-side cenote parks with rentals, guides, and spectacular caverns.

Gran Cenote: A lovely cavern with natural arches and stalactite formations, east of Tulum on the road to Cobá.

VALLADOLID
Cenote X'Canché: A pretty 12-meter-deep (39 feet) cenote, a kilometer (0.6 mile) down a forest path from Ek Balam ruins.

– Liza Prado and Gary Chandler, authors of *Moon Cancún & Cozumel, Moon Yucatán Peninsula,* and *Moon Chiapas*

Tulum, but it is far more important—and only receives a fraction of the visitors.

The Ruins
The **Cobá Group** welcomes visitors at the entrance with 50 structures, including the 22.5-meter-tall **La Iglesia,** the second-tallest pyramid in the city. (La Iglesia is off-limits to climbers.) Cobá has two well-preserved **ball courts** with grotesque death imagery. A pleasant and well-kept trail and bike route built atop the city's *sacbeob* takes you to the **xaibé.** Located at the end of the bike path, this building may have served as an astronomical observatory or watchtower.

Cobá's crown jewel is **Nohuch Mul**—at 12

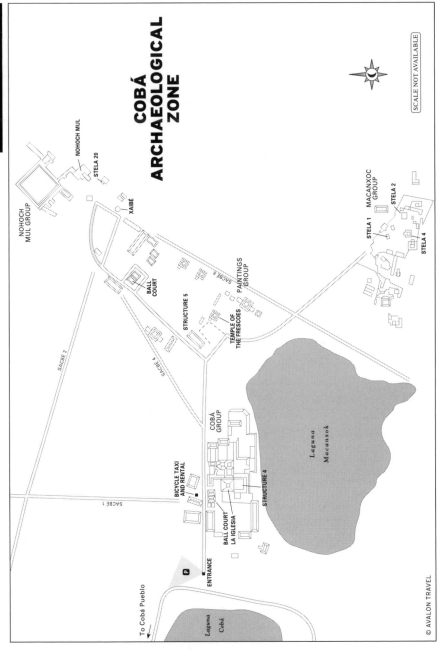

COBÁ ARCHAEOLOGICAL ZONE

SCALE NOT AVAILABLE

NOHOCH MUL GROUP

NOHOCH MUL

STELA 20

XAIBÉ

MACANXOC GROUP

STELA 2

STELA 1

STELA 4

BALL COURT

STRUCTURE 5

SACBE 8

PAINTINGS GROUP

TEMPLE OF THE FRESCOES

SACBE 2

SACBE 4

COBÁ GROUP

Laguna Macanxok

BICYCLE TAXI AND RENTAL

STRUCTURE 4

SACBE 1

BALL COURT

LA IGLESIA

P

ENTRANCE

To Cobá Pueblo

Laguna Cobá

© AVALON TRAVEL

© JOSHUA BERMAN

Cobá's Stela 1, with its "deep time" inscription, may be evidence that the Maya did *not* intend anything to end in the year 2012.

stories (42 meters) above the forest floor, it is one of the tallest pyramids in the Mundo Maya (only the temple at Calakmul in Campeche is taller). This *is* one of the temples you can climb (at least until 4 P.M.), and the view from the top stretches across the Yucatán.

Cobá reached its peak of power A.D. 600–900 and fell to the Itzá of Chichén Itzá around A.D. 1000. The last Long Count date recorded here is on **Stela 20** and corresponds with November 30, A.D. 780.

In addition to marking the creation date of the Long Count (4 Ahau 8 Kumku, or August 11, 3114 B.C.), Cobá is famous for a "deep time" inscription, a *long* Long Count date 19 levels beyond the *b'aktun* and thousands of years older than modern astronomers' estimate for the age of the universe. This date is found on **Stela 1** in the Macanxoc Group, about a half-mile walk from the Paintings Group, It is easy to miss between the bigger temples (look for a sign to Structure 5).

Save time for a visit to one of four **cenotes**

on the road southwest of Cobá: Choo-Ha, Tamcach-Ha, Multun-Ha, and Nohoch-Ha. Each costs a few dollars to enter and is well worth it.

Visiting the Site

Cobá is open 7 A.M.–5 P.M. daily. Entrance costs US$4 admission, plus US$4 for parking. It's a two-kilometer (1.2-mile) walk on flat ground to reach the Nohoch Mul pyramid. Or if it's very hot (which it often is), you can rent a bicycle or hire a local rickshaw driver (US$3–5 per hour) to pedal you there. Guides are available and charge around US$30 per group.

The various groups of structures at Cobá are dispersed throughout the forest, and there's no real order to follow when visiting. Watch your step, as the trails have many confusing off-shoots. Time your visit for the morning or late afternoon. Bird-watchers who show up when the gates open at 7 A.M. will be well rewarded. Bring plenty of water and bug spray, and wear comfortable shoes.

There are a number of accommodations in and around Cobá Pueblo, and more a half-hour up the road in Tulum, but there are few services at Cobá itself.

Getting There

Cobá is just west of **Tulum** and south of **Valladolid.** From Cancún or Playa del Carmen, drive south to Tulum, and look for a signed turnoff to the right. From Chichén Itzá, head toward Valladolid, then look for the road to Ixhil, which will take you to Cobá. From Chetumal or Belize, head north on Highway 307 toward Tulum, then look for the turnoff to Cobá.

From the Cancún airport, take a bus to Playa del Carmen (US$6) then to Tulum (US$2.80), a trip of almost 113 kilometers (70 mi) total. You can also hire a car and driver for the day in Cancún (US$60–70) or sign up for a day trip.

There are several daily buses that make the trip up Highway 307 from Chetumal, stopping in Tulum, Playa del Carmen, and Cancún only a few hours.

UXMAL

Uxmal is located 70 miles west of Chichén Itzá (and only an hour's drive from Mérida) and is considered one of the most beautifully designed cities in the Maya world. Uxmal was founded around A.D 500 and thrived during the late Classic period (late 9th century) when most of its construction was completed. Uxmal means "built three times," and it was indeed destroyed and rebuilt at least that often. Rich soils in the region allowed large populations to thrive at Uxmal, whose highest glory was in the Late Classic period (A.D. 875–900) before the Toltec overran it around A.D. 1000.

Soaring 125 feet (38 meters) with a unique elliptical base and curved corners, the **Pyramid of the Magician** is one of the first structures you see after passing through the visitors center. You can't climb it anymore, but you can walk around it to the **Nunnery Quadrangle.** Ronald Wright, author of

Time Among the Maya, called the Nunnery Quadrangle "one of the masterpieces of Maya design." Stephens described it as "a tranquil space, enclosed and calmed by the smooth ashlars of the palace walls."

From the Nunnery, walk through the ball court to the **Governor's Palace.** The surrounding structures are remarkable, built atop a long, even platform with carvings of feathered serpents and over 100 Chaac rain god masks. The Governor's Palace has a unique "throne inscription" hieroglyphic above the entrance, which also displays the zodiac constellations. Look for the two-headed **Jaguar Throne,** which John Lloyd Stephens found in 1841 (and wanted to carry out before realizing it was too heavy).

The **Great Pyramd,** located behind the Governor's Palace, towers 30 meters (100 feet) high—and you can still climb it. At the top is another large Chaac mask and several panels depicting scarlet macaws.

Visiting the Site

Uxmal is open 8 A.M.–5 P.M. daily. Entrance is US$15 children under 13 are free, and there are small fees for parking and using a camera. The cost includes the **Light and Sound Show** (7 P.M. Oct.–Apr.; 8 P.M. May–Sept.), which takes place in the evening at the ruins overlooking the Nunnery Quadrangle. Tour guides are available at the entrance and offer 90-minute walking tours for US$40–55 per group. There is a museum, and a visitors center has a gift shop, ATM, snack bar, and bookstore. A few excellent lodges and restaurants are located near the entrance, including **Villas Arqueológicas Uxmal** (tel. 997/974-6020, U.S. tel. 888/293-0293, www.villasarqueologicas.com.mx, US$80–150).

Getting There

Uxmal is 48 miles from **Mérida** and two hours from **Campeche.** To reach Uxmal by car, drive down Highway 261 into the heart of the Puuc Route.

Special **Puuc Route buses** (US$13, entry fees not included) leave Mérida's second-class

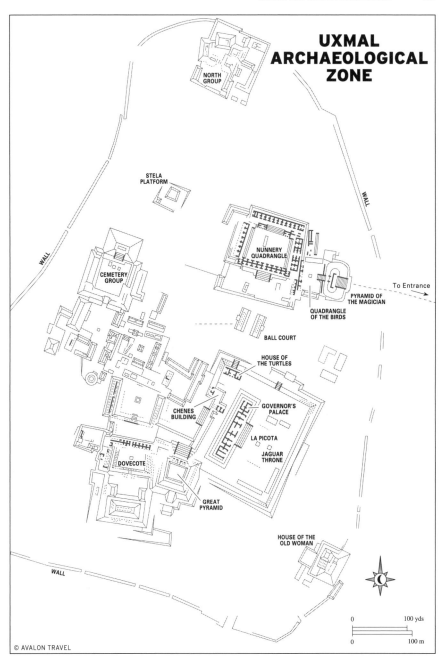

UXMAL ARCHAEOLOGICAL ZONE

NORTH GROUP

STELA PLATFORM

CEMETERY GROUP

NUNNERY QUADRANGLE

WALL

To Entrance

PYRAMID OF THE MAGICIAN

QUADRANGLE OF THE BIRDS

BALL COURT

HOUSE OF THE TURTLES

CHENES BUILDING

GOVERNOR'S PALACE

LA PICOTA

JAGUAR THRONE

DOVECOTE

GREAT PYRAMID

HOUSE OF THE OLD WOMAN

WALL

0   100 yds

0   100 m

© AVALON TRAVEL

bus terminal daily at 6 and 9 A.M. and spend 30 minutes each at Kabah, Sayil, and Labná, then two hours at Uxmal before returning to Mérida at 4 P.M. The adventurous can try ordinary public buses to get to and from Uxmal.

PALENQUE

The first time I heard of Palenque, I was in a cheap *hospedaje* in Managua, far south of Maya territory. I had not yet been to Mexico, Guatemala, or anywhere outside of Nicaragua, where I was stationed for two years as a Peace Corps Volunteer, so listening to tales of lost worlds from a freckled, blond Canadian backpacker made for inspiring travel dreams. She lit up as she talked about Palenque and struggled to describe the place, thus ensuring it a spot on my epic list. When she uttered the phrase "better than Tikal," the crowd in Hospedaje Santos hushed and turnedtheir heads.

Palenque (or "fortification") was so named in 1567 by the first Spaniard to glimpse its buildings peeking above the jungle on a hill above the Usumacinta River. Palenque was a small site, supporting perhaps 6,000 inhabitants, but it is a powerful and mysterious place. Palenque's importance lies "in its naturalistic sculpture, architectural inventiveness, and detailed epigraphic record," states Michael D. Carrasco, an assistant professor of art history at Florida State University.

Palenque was attacked by Calakmul in A.D. 599 and again in 611. A century later, Toniná sacked the city, but by A.D. 800 construction had stopped, and the city was abandoned soon after.

The Ruins

Palenque's multi-storied **Palace** is unparalleled in the Mundo Maya for its sheer size and height, as well as its maze of rooms, hallways, and carvings.

The **Temple of the Inscriptions** is home to one of the most amazing archaeological discoveries of the 20th century. Mexican archaeologist Alberto Ruz Lhuillier found a secret passageway under the temple stairs that led him to the tomb of Hanab-Pakal, Pakal the Great, one of the great kings of Palenque

who ruled in a successive dynasty of 17 rulers for over four centuries.

There are numerous "deep time" and future dates at Palenque, including one count that indicates 20, not 13, *b'aktuns* make up the Long Count cycle (which means the 2012-ers are off by 2,762 years). Several large branching World Tree images appear with quetzal birds. Other cross-like imagery is found in the **Temple of the Cross** and in nearby **South Group** (or Crosses Group), erected to mark the A.D. 684 ascension to the throne of Kan B'alam, or "Snake Jaguar." Archaeologists Linda Schele and David Friedel argue that this is symbolic of the Maya creation myth.

Temple XIII and the **Tomb of the Red Queen** are where Mexican archaeologists discovered the regal sarcophagus of a noblewoman; her remains and coffin were caked in red cinnabar. The **Temple of the Skull** actually only has one remaining skull, a bas-relief carving that is visible if you look up toward the top level. The temple was built atop several earlier ones, the oldest of which had a burial with an enormous jade offering.

Palenque's sole **ball court** was built around A.D. 500, a typical I-shape with low benches, now covered with neat grass. This is where Maya players once battled it out while reenacting their sacred creation myth.

Visiting the Site

Palenque is open 8 A.M.–5 P.M. daily. Entrance is US$5, or free after 4 P.M. Definitely save time for a visit to the **Museo Arqueológico de Palenque** (10 A.M.–4:30 P.M. Tues.–Sun.). The latest display is a reproduction of The Tomb of Pakal with a life-size reproduction of the sarcophagus.

There are plenty of places to stay in the area, including many *campamento* backpacker havens, Spartan budget hotels in Palenque town, or budget accommodations in the surrounding area, all specializing in Palenque tours. **Santo Domingo de Palenque** is located 8 kilometers (5 mi) from the entrance to Palenque. It is a basic town with the basic necessities for travelers and little else. The jungle community of

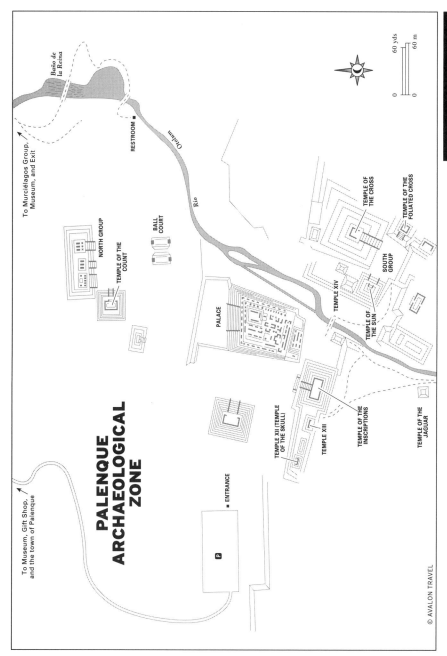

PALENQUE ARCHAEOLOGICAL ZONE

To Museum, Gift Shop, and the town of Palenque

To Murciélagos Group, Museum, and Exit

Baño de la Reina

RESTROOM

Río Otolum

NORTH GROUP

TEMPLE OF THE COUNT

BALL COURT

PALACE

TEMPLE XIV

SOUTH GROUP

TEMPLE OF THE CROSS

TEMPLE OF THE FOLIATED CROSS

TEMPLE OF THE SUN

ENTRANCE

P

TEMPLE XII (TEMPLE OF THE SKULL)

TEMPLE XIII

TEMPLE OF THE INSCRIPTIONS

TEMPLE OF THE JAGUAR

0   60 yds
0   60 m

© AVALON TRAVEL

Q&A: ALUNA JOY YAXK'IN, TRIP LEADER AND SPIRITUAL ARCHAEOLOGIST

"The best journey is made with the heart, not with a guidebook," said Aluna Joy Yaxk'in, author, guide, ordained minister, and "sacred site essence formulator." (Personally, I hope the best journey is a combination of these things, but I know what she means.) Aluna is a woman of many skills and hats, but with one essential mission: "To encourage others to recognize their own divinity," as she puts it. She uses her gifts to read the ancient history of sacred sites and has excellent advice for visiting them. Her website is www.AlunaJoy.com.

When did you first travel to the Mundo Maya? Where did you go and how did it impact you?
The first time I went to the Maya world was in 1986, and it completely changed my life. I received my first energy download on this trip, but I didn't understand it until many years later. I began to understand that the Maya lands had something to offer to everyone that enters these sacred sites. This is why I take groups there; and for myself, I have to go back at least once a year, if not more.

What advice do you have for someone traveling to a Maya village or archaeological site for the first time?
Before entering a sacred site, stop for a moment and ask permission to enter. Treat the place like it's a living being, because it is. If you don't feel a welcoming energy, it's not your time to enter. If you feel welcome, go with your heart wide open and filled with light. Walking in these places in thankfulness, in gratitude, and

in great respect opens many magical doors to wisdom that is anchored there. You will hear exactly what you need to hear; it won't be what other people hear. The sites speak to you personally. Be patient with yourself and know that it may take time to understand how it has shifted you. Most of all, have fun.

What does "responsible tourism" mean when traveling in the Mundo Maya?
Always journey to the Maya world with great respect for not only the country but the local traditions. That way, you'll elevate – not damage – the culture. If you go with the intent of helping, this can demean those you're trying to help. We always wait to be asked. I learned this the hard way.

We were traveling in Peru high in the Andes to visit some local Quechua villages. As a gesture of respect, we took food, coca leaf, oranges, and bread. We were handing them out to the children and the elders. I saw this one grandmother at a distance; she felt so powerful, I wanted to go meet her. I took a bag of coca leaf to her. She lit into me, with great passion and righteous anger, like you wouldn't believe. I didn't understand a word she said, but I got it. She didn't need me coming to her to give her coca leaf. She is perfectly capable of taking care of herself. She didn't need any part of the world I was coming from. By giving her coca leaf, which, by the way, for the most part is considered a sign of respect, I had unconsciously told her that I thought I was better than she. The truth was actually the other way around. I thought she was amazing. But she

El Panchan, on the edge of the entrance to ruins, is a better bet with a handful of hotels and restaurants.

In 2012
Visit on **summer solstice** (June 20) to witness the powerful lighting of the Temple of the Sun.

From 1998 through 2000, Dr. Edwin Barnhart, working with a team from the University of Texas at Austin, led a site-mapping project that identified and recorded 1,478 structures, most in the outlying city area. Barnhart, director of the Maya Exploration Center is leading several trips in 2012.

COURTESY OF ALUNA JOY YAXKIN

Aluna Joy at her favorite site, Palenque

didn't know this. In 60 seconds I learned an incredibly valuable lesson. Pay attention. Help when it is appropriate. Your heart will know the right time and place.

Do you have any travel plans in the year 2012?

We're going to Palenque and Yaxchilán in Mexico; Tikal and Quiriguá in Guatemala; and Copán in Honduras. These sites represent the five elements: earth, water, air, fire, and ether.

We are excited because I consider these the five crowns of light in the Maya world.

I would never suggest to anyone which site they should go to on December 21, 2012. This is something you need to decide for yourself. My favorite is Palenque in Mexico. Sometimes I think my heart lives there permanently. But each site speaks to people in different ways. So I would suggest finding pictures of all the Maya temples that you consider going to and seeing which one calls to you the strongest.

Getting There

Villahermosa is the closest city to Palenque and is located 93 miles northwest in the state of Tabasco. To reach Palenque, rent a car in Villahermosa or take a bus (US$9.50, 2.5 hrs). From San Cristóbal de las Casas, it's a four-hour drive to Palenque.

There is an ADO bus terminal about 100 meters (328 feet) from the entrance to the Palenque ruins with bus connections to Campeche, Cancún, Mérida, San Cristóbal, Villahermosa, and Mexico City. You can reach various sites in the Usumacinta Valley by *combi* (a shared public minibus) from Palenque town, including Bonampak, Frontera Corozal, and the Lacandón village of Lacanjá Chansayab.

YAXCHILÁN AND BONAMPAK
Yaxchilán

The large city of Yaxchilán (the name means "green stones") ruled the Usumacinta River valley in what is now the state of Chiapas, Mexico. At one point Yaxchilán was a major rival of Palenque, Piedras Negras (40 km down river), and Tikal. The city is known for its gorgeous views down the river, and for the detailed sculpture and well-preserved wooden lintel carvings above the temple doors. The sheer quantity of hieroglyphic writing found here has given Yaxchilán a reputation for being "a treasure trove for epigraphers."

Yaxchilán boasts the best-named founding father ever: Yat B'alam (Jaguar Penis), who took the throne in A.D. 320. The most important ruler of Yaxchilán, however, was Izamnaaj B'alam (Shield Jaguar), born in A.D. 647. Izamnaaj B'alam ruled for 60 years and built an enormous monument for his wife, Lady Xoc. **Structure 23,** on the main plaza, is the only Maya structure known to have been built for a woman. Look for the carved panel featuring Lady Xoc passing a thorn-studded rope through her tongue in blood ritual.

There is some Long Count evidence at Yaxchilán. On the ball game panels under **Temple 33** are some particularly deep Long Count texts—longer even than the 13 *b'aktun* cycle. The earliest important date written at the site is A.D. 435; the latest is A.D. 808.

Bonampak

Thirty kilometers (19 mi) south of Yaxchilán lies Bonampak, a separate site atop a beautiful ridge. It is famous for its brilliant color murals, painted around A.D. 800. Scenes depict a great, bloody battle in A.D. 792 and are fantastic for their detail, especially those located within **Structure 1** (The Temple of the Murals). A full-scale reproduction of the temple is in the National Museum of Anthropology and History in Mexico City. Bonampak is included in most tours to Yaxchilán.

Visiting the Sites

Yaxchilán is open 10 A.M.–5 P.M. daily, but accessible only by boat. Entrance is US$5. Team up with a tour company or find a boat service in the town of Frontera Corozal. After docking at the site, visitors enter a tunnel under Edificio 19 and emerge into the Grand Plaza. Instead of following the main path, climb to the Little Acropolis and work your way downhill through the ruins.

Most people visit Yaxchilán and Bonampak as a combined trip after touring Palenque, a four-hour drive down the river valley. Bonampak Archaeological Park is open 8 A.M.–5 P.M. daily. Entrance is US$10. There are basic services and refreshments at the visitors center.

The border town of Frontera Corozal was founded in 1976 by Ch'ol Maya immigrants from Guatemala and has some basic services, including boats and guides, a museum, restaurants, and accommodations like **Escudo Jaguar** (tel. 502/5353-5637, www.escudojaguarhotel.com, US$20–60).

Getting There

This is the best part: Yaxchilán can only be reached by a 25-kilometer *lancha* (boat) ride (45–60 min., US$65 for 1–3 passengers) from the village of **Frontera Corozal.**

By *combi* from Palenque, buses leave hourly 5 A.M.–5 P.M. (US$7). By car from Palenque, take the Carretera Fronteriza approximately 100 miles to Crucero Corozal. From there, drive 13.5 miles to Frontera Corozal.

IZAPA

This unassuming site in southwestern Mexico, in the shadow of Volcán Tacaná, was inhabited for nearly 3,000 years before finally being abandoned around A.D. 1200. Izapa's influence extended up and down the Pacific Coast, and it served as a powerful Preclassic city-state and trading center, dominating the area for a millennium. Izapa occupies an interesting place in history between the Middle Preclassic Olmecs and the Early Classic Maya.

Izapa is thought by some researchers to be a crucial place for the development of the sacred calendar. At the latitude of Izapa, the number of days in the sacred Tzolk'in calendar (260 days) is equal to the number of days between

Q&A: JOHN MAJOR JENKINS, AUTHOR

One of the top 2012 thinkers and authors about the phenomenon, John Major Jenkins believes that the Maya chose the date December 21, 2012, to coincide with the solstice sun aligning with the dark rift of the Milky Way – an event highly symbolic to the Maya's creation myth and cosmovision. Jenkins first described the galactic alignment theory in his book *Maya Cosmogenesis 2012: The True Meaning of the Maya Calendar End-Date*. His latest book, *The 2012 Story*, gives an incredibly thorough overview of the rare world of 2012ology, a body of thought that spans many disciplines, from astronomy and archeology to spirituality, mythology, and metaphysics.

When did you first travel to a Mundo Maya country and how did it impact you?
On a long trip in 1986 and 1987, funded by working the night shift in a factory for a year. I was 22. It was very important, and I returned in 1988, '89, '90, '94, and many times afterward. I realized that the Maya civilization understood astronomy in ways that we were just beginning to discover.

What advice do you have for someone travel-ing to a Maya village or archaeological site for the first time?
Take your time, wander around, take it all in. Get a sense of the space; take pictures and study the details later.

What has been your most memorable travel moment so far traveling in the Mundo Maya?
I have had many incredible heartwarming experiences with the Maya people, living and working in the highlands, and meeting interesting travelers from all over the world. My study of Izapa – the place that was involved in formulating the 2012 calendar – is also very important to me. (It is still largely ignored by mainstream academia, even though I was the first to identify and publish the ball court's alignment to the December solstice sunrise.)

Do you have any travel plans in the year 2012?
I'd suggest [traveling to] Izapa, of course; that would make sense. Copán in Honduras would be nice. I have made no plans for the December 21 day, but the whole year will be filled with events and presentations.

solar zenith passages (the two days of the year when the sun is exactly overhead). Because one of those days is August 13—the Gregorian calendar date that correlates with the beginning of the Long Count in 3114 B.C.—this may indicate that the Izapans also developed the Long Count.

The Ruins

Izapa is a small site, with about 80 temple mounds decorated with river rocks. Izapa's **ball court** points straight to the December solstice sunrise, and several **stelae** here have distinct images of frogs, caimans, the Hero Twins, and Wuqub Kaquix himself, the 7 Macaw underworld character from the sacred *Popol Vuh*. This mix of creation mythology and astronomy helped lead John Major Jenkins,

an independent researcher and author, to his galactic alignment theory; at its core is the Izapans' "awareness of the future galactic alignment in era-2012" when the sun will align with the dark rift in the Milky Way on the winter solstice. This theme is also present in the ball game; as the ball passes through the goal-ring, it signals the dawning of a new age.

Izapa is sure to be a central spot to visit for the winter solstice, considering that day's significance in the architecture and mythology of the place.

Visiting the Site

Izapa is open 8 A.M.–5 P.M. Wednesday through Sunday; there are no entrance fees. Izapa is not included on most tours. It is neither obvious nor easy to visit, but it is a must-see for hard-core

Maya *turistas*. **The Maya Conservancy** (http://mayaconservancy.org) is making a huge effort to bring some basic facilities to Izapa to highlight its importance.

Getting There

Izapa lies about 20 miles from the Pacific Ocean, just east of the city of **Tapachula.** Driving east from Tapachula, look for the Ruinas Izapa Restaurante. The main groups of structures are a short walk from this restaurant. You can also take a *combi* from Tapachula en route to Cacahoatán; ask to be let off at *las ruinas de Izapa*. The drive from town should take about half an hour and cost less than US$1.

You can reach Izapa from Guatemala, via the town of San Marcos in the Western Highlands, then continuing on to the border town of El Carmen. The road continues to Tapachula, Mexico, where there are Izapa transportation and guides.

Tours and Packages

Mexico offers a number of community tourism ventures in Maya villages, such as Muchucuxcah, throughout the Yucatán and in Chiapas. Ideally, such programs create a more attractive alternative for villagers who would otherwise have to leave the village to work in the big hotels along the coast. If thatch roofs and pit toilets are too primitive for your taste, *no hay problema*. There are plenty of colonial, Caribbean, and other Mexican towns and cities perfectly situated for Maya-centered excursions, all with accommodations for every budget and long lists of day trips. Accommodations options range from theme parks and high-rises in the mass tourist destinations around Cancún and the Riviera Maya, to converted haciendas along Mérida, to memorable bed-and-breakfasts along the coast near Tulum.

COMMUNITY TOURISM
AlltourNative Offtrack Adventures

AlltourNative (tel. 877/437-4990, www.alltour native.com), just south of Cancún, offers exciting Maya-theme day trips around the state of Quintana Roo. They have longstanding relationships with Maya villages near cenotes and other sites and can customize a responsible tourism plan for your travels. Their **Cobá Maya Encounter Expedition** is an all-day trip that begins in Cobá and includes a number of other local adventure activities (US$119 per person).

El Hombre Sobre La Tierra

El Hombre Sobre La Tierra (tel. 999/927-0719, info@elhombresobrelatierra.org, http://elhombresobrelatierra.org) works with communities in Yucatán and Campeche with the broader mission of promoting environmental sustainability and food self-sufficiency, and advancing the integration of women in the economy. These are all in play in the eco-tourism project in the village of **Muchucuxcah** (you can say it, it's fun actually: "Moo-choo-KOOSH-kah"). Visiting service groups help construct an infrastructure that invites travelers to stay in their community. They call it *el turismo solidario*—solidarity tourism. Guests sleep in hammocks strung inside traditionally built *palapas* and take meals with families in the community.

Intercambio Cultural Maya

For decades, the Maya Cultural Exchange (tel. 812/232-0186, www.intercambio-maya.org, US$1,095 per person per trip) has organized visits twice annually to different Maya villages, inviting doctors, nurses, dentists, pharmacists, translators, and volunteers to help run free medical/dental clinics. They also build community-directed public works projects for the village (hurricane shelters or other community buildings). Volunteers stay in the homes of Maya families.

© JOSHUA BERMAN

There are several community tourism opportunities in the Mexican Mundo Maya.

Moots Prehispanic Art School

The Moots Prehispanic Art School (tel. 984/134-7966, agusbarro@yahoo.com.ar) is run by Augustín Villalba, an Argentinian teacher who has been living in Maya villages for five years. Villalba arranges volunteer project and primitive lodging in the Tres Reyes village school; he can also help distribute any contributions.

Consider buying some pottery from the art school shop; 100 percent of the proceeds go to this important educational program. (The craft shop is to the left across from the crocodile-feeding dock, one block before the entrance to Cobá.)

Yaxunah

Yaxunah Centro Cultural (http://yaxunahcentrocultural.org or http://mayaresearchprogram.org) is a small indigenous community 20 miles from **Chichén Itzá** and Pisté with a unique grassroots village tourism opportunity. They welcome visitors to the community, especially volunteers who would like to share their skills

with groups in the village (help document the flora of the area or teach ESL or computer classes to youth). Swim in the local cenote and tour the cultural interpretive center and gardens, or stay for a week to teach art classes, embroidery, or dance, or to plant trees.

TOURS IN 2012
Archaeological Tours

Archaeological Tours (tel. 212/986-3054 or 866/740-5130, www.archaeologicaltrs.com) has one academic Mexico trip planned in 2012: **Lords of the River and the Plains: The Northern Maya Kingdoms** (16 days, Jan. 6–21, US$5,500 per person), led by Professor William Saturno, a professor of anthropology at Boston University. This thorough trip covers the major sites of the Yucatán, then spends several days in Palenque before continuing west to San Cristóbal de las Casas.

Casa Frederick Catherwood

The Casa Frederick Catherwood (Mérida,

tel. 999/165-5565, info@casa-catherwood.
com, www.casa-catherwood.com) plans three
2012: A New Katun Begins tours: "Path
to Enlightenment" (5 days, Mar.
20–25, US$1,400 per person); "A Holistic Life" (5
days, June 19–24, US$1,650 per person); and
"Rebirth and Renewal" (6 days, Sept.
18–23, US$1,950 per person). These trips of "enlight-
enment and self-discovery" will be led by Don
Emilio Guadalupe Chan, a Maya spiritual
leader.

Casa K'in

In Mérida, Casa K'in (tel. 999/924-3176, info@
casakin.org, www.casakin.org) is offering **13
Maya Wisdom Intensives,** one each month
starting in January 2012. Led by Miguel Angel
Vergara, an author and expert on Chichén Itzá
and Maya culture, each intensive is different;
together they form a program for the end of
the old era and the beginning of the new.
These workshops will focus on Chichén Itzá,
Uxmal, Mayapan, Labna, Palenque, Yaxchilán,
Chikana, Edzna, Tulum, and Cobá.

Green Parrot Tours

Green Parrot Tours (tel. 999/901-5430, U.S.
tel. 214/329-9754, www.yucatandaytours.
com) offers special day tours of **Izamal,** and
to the workshops and homes of Maya artisans,
including a wood carver, a hammock-making
family, a textile family, and a jeweler.

Kenosis Spirit Keepers

In Chiapas, Kenosis Spirit Keepers (www.
kenosisspiritkeepers.org) offers the **Entering
the Maya Mysteries** program (12 days, Jan.
13–25). This immersion program brings Hopi
leaders from the north to engage with their
Maya cousins. Visitors are invited to support the program and to participate in the
ceremonies.

Maya Exploration Center

The Maya Exploration Center (MEC, tel.
512/350-3321, www.mayaexploration.org)
offers an **Ancient Maya Calendars and
Astronomy: Spring Equinox 2012 Tour**

(Mar. 17–26, US$2,800 per person) with visits
to Chichén Itzá, Dzibilchaltun, Uxmal, Tulum,
Cobá, and Ek Balam. Led by anthropologist Dr.
Michael Grofe, the tours include lectures about
the Maya calendar and ancient astronomy, and
what to believe about 2012. Special guest lec-
turers include archaeo-astronomer Felipe Chan
Chi, who will explain his 20 years of research
at Dzibilchaltun's Temple of the Seven Dolls;
and Sid Hollander, who wrote the world's first
Maya to Gregorian calendar conversion soft-
ware. Finally, you'll stand beneath Chichén
Itzá's Castillo Pyramid as the shadow snake
descends on March 20, the spring equinox.
Prices include lodging, transportation, entry
fees, breakfasts, MEC anthropologist guide,
four lectures, and the final dinner.

Mayan Ecotours

Mayan Ecotours (tel. 999/987-3710, mayan-
ecotours@hotmail.com, www.mayanecotours.
com) has a special trip throughout 2012: the
chance to receive a purification from a Maya
priest at a special altar set up in a cave. The
goal, they explain, "is to be rid of your fears,
guilt, and any negativity that damages the
mind, body, and spirit." This tour (day or night
available, US$80) includes transport, guides,
helmets and flashlights, the Maya ceremony,
and a typical dinner afterward, with a big shot
of *xtabentún,* the ancient Maya's anise liqueur
made with fermented honey.

MayaSites Travel

Two of the Traveling in Maya Time 2012 Solstice
Trips offered by travel specialists MayaSites
Travel (tel. 877/620-8715, mayasites@yahoo.
com, www.mayasites.com) are entirely in Mexico.
Guests fly into Cancún for the **Beginning the
New Calendar Era Under the Yucatán Stars**
tour (5 nights, Dec. 17–22, US$1,520 per person
based on double occupancy), a celebration of the
beginning of a new Maya calendar cycle with
visits to the sites of Tulum, Cobá, Ek Balam,
Chichén Itzá, Dzibilchaltun, Cenote Ik Kil,
and the colonial cities of Valladolid and Mérida.
The tour includes a gala dinner and count-
down to 2012. Prices include lodging, ground

transportation, entry and guide fees, breakfast, one lunch, and one gala dinner.

The Temples of Maya Calendar Inscriptions tour (5 nights, Dec. 18–23, US$1,475 per person based on double occupancy) is based out of Villahermosa. Guests ring in the next 13 *b'aktuns* with tours of Palenque, Yaxchilán, Bonampak, and La Venta Olmec Museum.

Sacred Earth Journeys

Sacred Earth Journeys (tel. 604/874-7922 or 877/874-7922, info@sacredearthjourneys. ca, www.sacredearthjourneys.ca), based in Vancouver, British Columbia, offers a 10-day **Maya Sacred Path to 2012** tour (Nov. 29–Dec. 8), beginning and ending in Villahermosa, Mexico. One of the trip leaders is Don Miguel Angel Vergara Calleros, who has been "studying, teaching, and living the Maya wisdom for over 25 years." In addition to visiting important Maya and Olmec sites, this trip explores "the lost cultures of Lemuria and Atlantis" and provides a chance to meet local Olmec elders, Maya shaman, priests, priestesses, and teachers.

Tia Stephanie Tours

Tia Stephanie Tours (tel. 734/769-7839, info@ tiastephanietours.com, www.tiastephanietours. com) is a U.S.-based tour operator that specializes in cultural and educational travel programs throughout Mexico. There are two special tours offered in 2012.

The **Maya Calendar and Glyph Workshop** (8 days, Jan. 5–13, US$1,875 per person, double occupancy) will be led by Dr. Gabrielle Vail, PhD, adjunct assistant professor of anthropology at New College of Florida. Dr. Vail specializes in Maya iconography and hieroglyphic texts. The fundamentals of Maya writing (epigraphy) and the Maya calendar will be explained in classroom-style settings. Participants are then led into the field for further learning at Palenque, Bonampak, Yaxchilán, and Tonina. Visits include the city of San Cristóbal de las Casas and the highland Maya communities of Chamula and Zinacantan.

Tia Stephanie is also offering **Maya and 2012: The End of Time?** (8 days, Aug. 11–18,

US$1,785 per person, double occupancy), developed by Dr. David S. Anderson, PhD, from Tulane University. Dr. Anderson is an archaeologist currently researching the Preclassic period of the northern lowland Maya. This tour provides an introduction to the Maya calendar, writing, astronomy, politics, divine kingship, and royal succession, and includes class work and archaeological visits throughout the Yucatán.

Chocolate Tours

In Mérida, chocolate maker **Ki' Xocolatl** (www.ki-xocolatl.com) has a four-day culinary adventure they call The Great Cacao Expedition. This unique chocolate-intensive tour includes chocolate cooking workshops in a colonial mansion, visits to Maya ceremonial cities, and a day at a cacao and spice plantation. You'll stay in Casa San Ángel, a boutique hotel on the Paseo de Montejo, and dine at fancy remodeled haciendas. Ki' Xocolatl runs a chocolate museum full of artifacts and tools used in cacao preparation and chocolate-making.

Also in Mérida, **Casa Frederick Catherwood** (tel. 999/165-4986, info@casacatherwood.com, www.casa-catherwood. com) offers the Great Chocolate Expedition, an intensive five-day trip that includes cooking classes and trips to Maya sites and the Tikul cacao plantation, also in conjunction with Ki' Xocolatl.

MexicaChica Getaways (tel. 999/901-5430, U.S. tel. 214/329-9754, www.mexicachica.com) is offering several five-day 2012 Chocolate Expeditions (Oct. 8–12, 2011 and Feb. 18–22, 2012, US$1,200 per person based on double occupancy). It includes visits to archaeological sites and tours of a cacao plantation and a museum.

HOTEL PACKAGES
Riviera Maya

The Maya of the Yucatán once undertook ritual canoe voyages to the island of Cutzamil (now Cozumel) to honor Ixhcel, the goddess of the moon. On the third weekend in May, 2012, **Xcaret** (toll-free Mex. tel. 800/212-

© JOSHUA BERMAN

The Mayan Sacred Journey will be reenacted at Xcaret on the Riviera Maya.

8951, toll-free U.S. tel. 888/922-7381, www. xcaret.com or www.travesiasagradamaya.com. mx) will host the **Mayan Sacred Journey,** the sixth annual reenactment of this 34-mile journey by canoe, made by hundreds of costumed paddlers and overseen by Maya priests. Over a period of three days, canoes depart before dawn, receive their blessing from Ixchel on the island, then arrive on the beach in Playa del Carmen. This impressive event begins with the recreation of a live marketplace filled with Yucatec-speaking vendors and continues with a series of dance, music, and theater productions for each launching and blessing of the canoes.

Xcaret is an eco-archaeological park built around several cenotes and underground rivers. Xcaret also offers tours to archaeological sites and Maya villages, focusing on Maya cuisine and crafts. Their Cobá Sunset mountain bike tour through the Cobá ruins includes a Maya crafts break, a traditional dinner with live music, and a Maya ball game inside a cenote.

Chichén Itzá

Just before Christmas 2011, **Mayaland Resorts** (tel. 800/235-4079, www.mayaland. com) will begin hosting a year-long series of 50 symposiums conducted by Maya scholars, authors, and religious leaders. Hosted on the doorsteps of Chichén Itzá and Uxmal in the Yucatán, these free symposiums are organized for tourists and locals alike and aim to impart a deeper understanding of Maya culture—including the Maya calendar. Scheduled topics include "What the Future Will Hold Beyond 2012," "Sex and the Maya," "Maya Medicine," and "Cuisine of the Maya." The wide-ranging symposiums will culminate on December 21, 2012, with an event at **Uxmal,** a city known as the Mecca of the Maya.

Xcanatun (tel. 888/883-3633, www.xcana-tun.com) also has trips to the villages of Ek Balam and Yaxunah, both close to Chichén Itzá. Eat a traditional Maya lunch with villagers, hit a ceremonial center at Uxmal, swim in a cenote, then tour Chichén Itzá itself. At the end of the day, expect a Maya-theme spa treatment and gourmet meal.

Mérida

Hacienda Xcanatun (tel. 888/883-3633, www.xcanatun.com, US$260–360 per night) is owned by Jorge Ruz, son of famous Mexican Maya archaeologist Alberto Ruz Lhuillier who discovered King Pakal's tomb in Palenque. A restored 18th-century *sisal* hacienda outside Mérida, Xcanatun offers three day trips in honor of the Year of the Maya; each full-day tour is in an air-conditioned vehicle with a trained guide. Guests visit the semi-excavated sites of Mayapan (35 miles southeast of Mérida) or Chacmultun (90 miles southeast of Mérida); or travel to the ancient Maya salt mines via horseback or kayak and throw in a bird-watching tour of the Río Lagartos Biosphere.

In 2012, **Hotel Caribe** and **La Mision de Fray** (tel. 999/924-9022, U.S. tel. 888/822-6431, www.hotelcaribe.com.mx) are offering a 15–20 percent discount off tours to Uxmal-Kabah, the Uxmal Light and Sound show, and Chichén Itzá. Room rates will also be discounted. Either hotel makes an excellent base for exploration.

Palenque

Boutique Hotel Quinta Chanabnal (tel. 916/345-5320, reservacion@quintachanabnal.com, www.quintachanabnal.com) is just a few miles from the entrance to Palenque. Owner Raphael Tunesi says his obsession with Maya culture began when he was 12. Since then, Italian-born Tunesi, an internationally recognized scholar and author, has visited nearly every reachable Maya site in the Mundo Maya. Palenque is one of his favorites (maybe because that's where he met his wife). Starting in the summer of 2012 and running through the end of the year, guests at Quinta Chanabnal will be able to take part in morning workshops on the Maya calendar, religion, and culture led by the multilingual Tunesi. Guests will then tour Palenque, where that morning's learning will be put to use at the actual site.

Also starting in the summer of 2012 and running through the end of the year, the hotel will offer special tours throughout the Mundo Maya to ruins most connected with the Maya Long Count Calendar and 2012. Tours are open to guests and nonguests and include Tikal, Toniná, Yaxchilán, and Cobá.

GUATEMALA

My first morning in Tikal, I woke up at least an hour before my alarm went off, with anticipatory endorphins surging through my hungry traveler's veins. Tikal at sunrise! I'd made it! I stepped out to look at the stars, then dressed and packed my camera bag. After taking a cold shower, I went out looking for the main gate to the park. I was not alone.

As the sky turned from gray to blue, a crowd gathered at the park entrance. Two Guatemalan guards with shotguns stood their ground as tourists from around the world begged to enter the park.

"¡Por favorrrr!"

"We came from the other side of the world!" cried a young woman in proper Castilian Spanish. "For the sunrise!"

The soldiers' faces remained unmoved, jungle versions of the Queen's Guards.

I knew that the days when travelers were allowed to sleep under the stars atop the temples of Tikal were long gone. But I was still surprised at the punctuality of the 6 A.M. opening, here in the middle of the wilderness, where rules were usually more flexible.

I decided to play it *suave*. "Is it like this every day?" I asked one of the guards, shaking my head in sympathy and gesturing to the sniveling crowd with my head. He smirked and nodded. We were buddies, *si*.

"Can you just give me a little *pasadita*?" I asked, and flashed my press card. "I need some pictures for a magazine article." It was true.

"No, man," he answered.

© AL ARGUETA

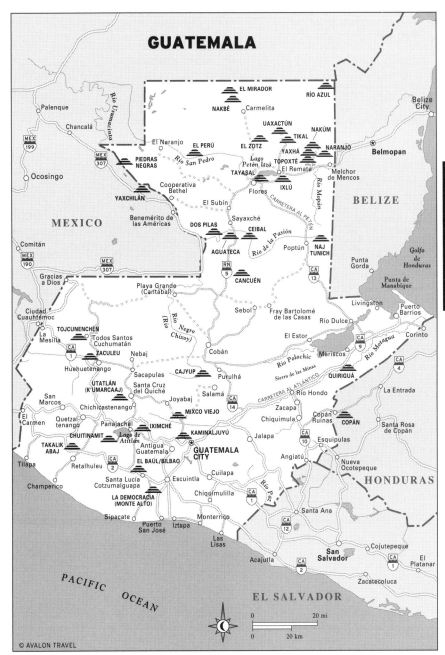

GUATEMALA

GUATEMALA

MEXICO

BELIZE

HONDURAS

EL SALVADOR

Palenque
Chancalá
MEX 199
Ocosingo
MEX 307
Comitán
MEX 190
Gracias a Dios
Ciudad Cuauhtémoc
La Mesilla
MEX 307
Río Usumacinta

El Naranjo
PIEDRAS NEGRAS
YAXCHILÁN
Cooperativa Bethel
Benemérito de las Américas
Río San Pedro
EL PERÚ
El Subín
DOS PILAS
AGUATECA
RN 5
CANCUÉN

EL MIRADOR
NAKBÉ Carmelita
UAXACTÚN
EL ZOTZ **TIKAL**
YAXHÁ
Lago Petén Itzá **TOPOXTÉ**
TAYASAL El Remate
Flores **IXLÚ**
CARRETERA AL PETÉN
Sayaxché
CEIBAL
Río de la Pasión
Poptún **NAJ TUNICH**
CA 13

RÍO AZUL
NAKÚM
NARANJO
Melchor de Mencos
Río Mopán

Belize City
Belmopan
Golfo de Honduras
Punta Gorda
Punta de Manabique

Playa Grande (Cantabal)
Sebol
Fray Bartolomé de las Casas
Río Dulce
Livingston
Puerto Barrios
Corinto
CA 9

Río Negro (Río Chixoy)
TOJCUNENCHÉN
Todos Santos Cuchumatán
ZACULEU Nebaj
CA 1
Huehuetenango
Sacapulas
UTATLÁN (K'UMARCAAJ)
Santa Cruz del Quiché
CAJYUP Purulhá
Cobán
El Estor
Mariscos
Río Polochic
Sierra de las Minas
QUIRIGUÁ
La Entrada
CA 4
Río Motagua

San Marcos
El Carmen
Quetzaltenango
Chichicastenango
Joyabaj
Salamá
CA 14
MIXCO VIEJO
Río Hondo
CARRETERA AL ATLÁNTICO
Zacapa
Chiquimula
Copán Ruinas
COPÁN
Santa Rosa de Copán
Esquipulas
CA 10

Panajachel
CHUITINAMIT
IXIMCHÉ
Lago de Atitlán
KAMINALJUYÚ
Antigua Guatemala
GUATEMALA CITY
Jalapa
Angiatú
Nueva Ocotepeque

TAKALIK ABAJ
Tilapa
Retalhuleu
EL BAÚL/BILBAO
CA 2
Cuilapa
Escuintla
Río Paz

Champerico
Santa Lucía Cotzumalguapa
Chiquimulilla
CA 1
Santa Ana
Santa Ana

LA DEMOCRACIA (MONTE ALTO)
Sipacate
Puerto San José
Iztapa
Monterrico
CA 12
San Salvador
CA 2
Cojutepeque
El Platanar
CA 1

Las Lisas
Acajutla
Zacatecoluca

PACIFIC OCEAN

0   20 mi
0   20 km

© AVALON TRAVEL

Q&A: ROBERT SITLER, PHD, AUTHOR

"The lessons that we non-Maya stand to learn from the living Maya," writes Dr. Robert Sitler, author and professor of modern languages and director of Stetson University's Latin American Studies program in DeLand, Florida, "are not esoteric messages from the stars or complex prophecies hidden in hieroglyphic texts that we must struggle to interpret." On the contrary, he writes in his book, *The Living Maya: Ancient Wisdom in the Era of 2012*, "they are gems of wisdom drawn from thousands of years of human experience." For his part, Dr. Sitler draws from at least 30 years of travel in Guatemala, Mexico, and Belize, where he has made many friends over the years. Currently, he is investigating what the Maya in the Chiapas highlands think about the future, particularly about the year 2012.

When did you first travel to the Mundo Maya? Where did you go and how did it impact you?
I first traveled to the Mundo Maya in the mid-1970s among the Ch'ol and Tzeltal peoples of Chiapas. The experience was radically transformative in that it reframed my understanding of what it meant to have a satisfying life. In particular I noticed the highly nurturing ways in which babies are raised, virtually living as an appendage of their mothers for the first year or two of their lives. This struck me as key to the generalized psychological well-being among the Maya villagers we met.

What advice do you have for someone traveling to a Maya village or archaeological site for the first time?
As far as visiting Maya communities, I would very strongly recommend doing some research beforehand, particularly concerning which of the 30 Mayan languages is spoken in the area where you plan to visit. At least learn basic greetings and phrases of courtesy. Dress and behave modestly so as to avoid offending people's sensibilities. Do not take photos of people unless they encourage you to do so or until after you know people well enough to ask permission and always send them the image in the mail.

As far as visiting archaeological sites, I would not recommend hiring a guide. Few on-site guides have access to up-to-date and accurate information on the site. Instead, you

---

I didn't push it. Finally, he raised the gate and stood aside, allowing the Kentucky Derby of backpackers to take off into the forest. My traveling companion, a fellow amateur photojournalist, and I had just completed a season working as firefighters for the U.S. National Park Service. We were in good shape and we quickly pulled ahead of the pack, speedwalking through the trees as birds and monkeys woke around us. We soon entered a labyrinth of structures, angling our way toward the Mundo Perdido Temple, where, according to a crusty expat in El Remate, there would be no other tourists.

"Everybody goes to Temple IV," he told us through a beer-foam mustache at the hotel bar. "But you'll have the Mundo Perdido all to yourselves."

He was right. As we ascended the steep, slick steps we had a few minutes to catch our breath and congratulate ourselves before the sun awoke beneath the mist. Low clouds illuminated and lifted. A mile away across the canopy, a multitude of insect-sized figures gathered at the highest steps of Temple IV. They felt far away even though their voices skimmed lightly across the trees.

As the dew dropped from the tree branches, the sun beamed across it all—the scene changing every second. We scurried back and forth with our tripods atop the Temple of the Lost World. We didn't talk, but we smiled and pointed and snapped away as the light and clouds and forest continued their morning show.

Guatemala is about such magic moments amid its grand temples—whether at sunrise,

© RIGOBERTO ITZEP/COURTESY OF ROBERT SITLER

Dr. Robert Sitler in Momostenango, Guatemala

can now find high-quality information in recent books and on academic online websites.

Do you know of any specific places or programs, especially community-based tourism efforts, that empower Maya villagers?
I highly recommend the efforts of the TEA, the Toledo Ecotourism Association, in southern Belize. This is a great way to learn about Maya cultures from within the communities. Numerous villages in Mexico now control tourist activities in their areas. I am unaware of any in Guatemala who do so. Always obey their rules and be respectful.

Do you have any travel plans in the year 2012?
I'm sure the ancient Maya would have considered [December 21, 2012] to be a very significant date. I do not think any particular world events will happen in association with the date. But I like to celebrate, so we'll probably do something special. We've been considering either the highest point in the Cuchumatan Mountains in Guatemala or Palenque, our favorite archaeological site.

sunset, or any time of day. The country boasts some of the world's most remarkable archaeological sites from all early periods of Maya life. But more than anything, Guatemala is the true heartland of Maya culture.

HISTORY

The early history of Guatemala's Maya is similar to that of Mexico. That is, hunters and gatherers as far back as 13,000 B.C. eventually adopted agriculture and settled village life by about 2,000 B.C. From there, things begin to diverge a bit between the two countries, based mostly on the physical environments in which pre-Maya and Maya populations found themselves.

There is enormous geographical and physical variation between the Yucatán lowlands and highland life in Guatemala. In Guatemala, for instance, the Maya produced and traded objects like jade, obsidian, and quetzal feathers with other populations to the north and east who desired them; these centers of trade helped the Preclassic Guatemalan Maya to further develop through the year A.D. 250 and into their Classic Period glory. By this time, dense population centers had been well established, especially in the northern Petén where Tikal's influence and power steadily grew.

Then came the great collapse around A.D. 900, which saw a widespread abandonment of the cities. For the next few centuries, surviving Maya fled north into the Yucatán, while others arrived from what is now Chiapas into the western Guatemalan high country. The K'iche', Tz'utujil, and Kaqchikel Maya groups battled it out over this time, until the arrival of the Europeans in the 16th century forced the warring Maya to unite against the bearded invaders. They put up a good fight but by 1527 were finally defeated, their leaders burned at the stake.

For those Maya that survived the diseases and new social order of the conquistadors, 500 years of continued subjugation, repression, and violence followed, much of it based on the land ownership system established by the Spanish when they arrived in Guatemala, which stripped the indigenous majority of their rights and consolidated land, cash crops, and control of the labor force (i.e., impoverished Maya) in the hands of a few light-skinned outsiders.

This condition continued up to and through the establishment of Guatemala as a sovereign nation in 1821 and into the mid-20th century. The people had just begun to make some progress, choosing their first democratically elected leader, Colonel Jacobo Árbenz Guzmán, who had promised land reform, but the United States deposed him in a secret CIA-sponsored 1954 coup d'etat. In his place, they helped install and train a brutal dictatorship, which, though violent toward the poor Maya majority of Guatemala, was amenable to the rights of the United Fruit Company and other foreign interests. What followed was a 36-year period known alternately as the Guatemalan Civil War or, simply, *la violencia.* As many as 200,000 Maya were killed, 40,000 disappeared, and up to a million displaced.

This act of genocide served to shatter the Maya people's connection with their land. Maya who are forced to live in a city or camp, unable to grow corn for their family, are effectively disconnected from their roots and culture. After Rigoberta Menchú was awarded the 1992 Nobel Peace Prize, her testimonials received global attention. In 1995, historic peace accords promised an end to the state-sponsored violence and allowed the Maya to practice their culture. Still, Guatemala continues to heal from many decades of war.

Just as the Spanish followed their initial conquest with the forcible introduction of Catholicism, so did the 1970s and 1980s see a massive invasion of proselytizing evangelical Protestants in Guatemala. Many of these groups, traveling in matching "prayer mission" T-shirts, continue to convert the indigenous population.

Today, the Maya of Guatemala are participating in the Maya culture revival. Nevertheless, more than half of Guatemala's Maya live in poverty and struggle day by day to feed their families.

PLANNING YOUR TIME

Mundo Maya International Airport (FRS) in **Santa Elena,** near Flores, is the only domestic airport in the country and is important for anyone exploring the sites of **Tikal, Uaxactún,** and **Yaxhá.** Santa Elena is also a good base for side trips into Belize. Contact **TACA** (tel. 502/2279-5645, www.taca.com) or **Transportes Aéreos Guatemaltecos** (tel. 502/2380-9401, www.tag.com.gt) for flight schedules.

The sprawling, hectic capital of **Guatemala City** makes a perfect starting point not only for Maya-focused travels within the country, but for multi-country tours as well. Many groups fly into Guatemala City and make side trips across the border to Copán, Honduras; to sites in Belize; and across the western border to the important but remote site of Izapa, Mexico.

From *la capital,* many travelers head straight to **Lake Atitlán** and the Western Highlands. The natural beauty of this area—with its soaring volcanoes, tranquil lake, and lush highlands—would be enough, but the region is also renowned as an indigenous stronghold, where Maya shamans and families still keep the calendars and ancient ways in villages like Quetzaltenango, Huehuetenango, and Momostenango. This is the Cuchumatan Mountains, the highest range in all of Central America, where there are sure to be numerous celebrations in 2012, all the way through the winter solstice.

In 2012

Guatemala's **Comité 2012 Guatemala** (www.2012guatemala.com) is a multi-agency government entity with the mission of leading a national movement around the ending of the 13 *b'aktun* Maya calendar cycle. Goals include the appreciation of Maya culture and the positioning of Guatemala as the true heartland of the Maya world and "fountain of spiritual inspiration for all of humanity." Amen. Events include Waqxaqi' B'atz': Día del Guía Espiritual (Day of the Spiritual Guide), a celebration of the end of the 260-day calendar, and B'eleje' B'atz' (Celebration of the Maya Women) in the Western Highlands.

Maya Archaeological Sites

Guatemala's archaeological and historical sites are managed by the government's **Instituto de Antropología e Historia** (IDAEH, Institute of Anthropology and History, www.mcd.gob. gt). IDAEH is part of the Ministry of Culture and Sports.

After visiting scores of sites across the Mundo Maya, journalists Karen Catchpole and Eric Mohl of the Trans-Americas Journey reported, "The grounds of the Maya sites in Guatemala are extremely well kept. We watched busy, busy caretakers sweep the paths at Yaxhá. Even remote and rarely visited sites like Dos Pilas were totally raked and clean." Camping is allowed at many sites in Guatemala; entrance to Yaxhá includes two free nights of camping on raised *palapa*-roofed platforms with views of the lake.

TIKAL

Tikal was the first-ever UNESCO World Heritage Site declared in the Mundo Maya. The archaeological zone is within Tikal National Park, a wildlife preserve that covers more than 64 square kilometers (25 sq mi) of pure Petén forest. In Yucatec Mayan, Tikal

© ZAPICHIGO/WWW.123RF.COM

Temple 1, The Great Jaguar

THE RUINS OF TIKAL

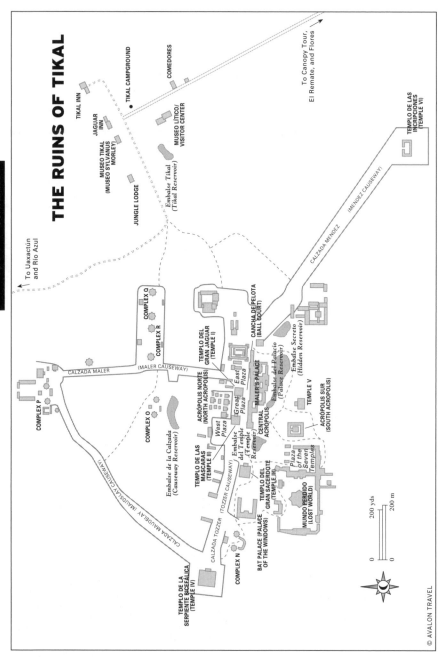

To Uaxactún
and Río Azul

TIKAL INN

JAGUAR INN

MUSEO TIKAL
(MUSEO SYLVANUS
MORLEY)

JUNGLE LODGE

TIKAL CAMPGROUND

COMEDORES

MUSEO LÍTICO/
VISITOR CENTER

Embalse Tikal
(Tikal Reservoir)

To Canopy Tour,
El Remate, and Flores

TEMPLO DE LAS
INCRIPCIONES
(TEMPLE VI)

CALZADA MENDEZ   (MÉNDEZ CAUSEWAY)

COMPLEX Q

COMPLEX R

CANCHA DE PELOTA
(BALL COURT)

CALZADA MALER   (MALER CAUSEWAY)

TEMPLO DEL
GRAN JAGUAR
(TEMPLE I)

ACRÓPOLIS NORTE
(NORTH ACROPOLIS)

COMPLEX P

COMPLEX O

East
Plaza

Great
Plaza

MALER'S PALACE

Embalse del Palacio
(Palace Reservoir)

Embalse Secreto
(Hidden Reservoir)

CENTRAL
ACROPOLIS

TEMPLE V

ACRÓPOLIS SUR
(SOUTH ACROPOLIS)

Embalse de la Calzada
(Causeway Reservoir)

TEMPLO DE LAS
MÁSCARAS
(TEMPLE II)

West
Plaza

Embalse
del Templo
(Temple
Reservoir)

Plaza
of the
Seven
Temples

TEMPLO DEL
GRAN SACERDOTE
(TEMPLE III)

MUNDO PERDIDO
(LOST WORLD)

CALZADA MAUDSLAY (MAUDSLAY CAUSEWAY)

(TOZZER CAUSEWAY)

CALZADA TOZZER

BAT PALACE (PALACE
OF THE WINDOWS)

COMPLEX N

TEMPLO DE LA
SERPIENTE BICEFÁLICA
(TEMPLE IV)

0   200 yds

0   200 m

© AVALON TRAVEL

means either "at the waterhole" or "place of the voices." Whatever definition you choose, Tikal has occupied a near mythical status on Central American traveler's trails for decades. The site is worth the hype.

Tikal was first reported by a westerner in 1695. A Spaniard priest was near starvation when he stumbled upon one of the greatest sites in the New World. Tikal's origins date back to at least 600 B.C., but the site's greatest structures were erected during the late Preclassic through the end of the Classic Periods. The ruins weren't excavated and restored until the University of Pennsylvania and Guatemalan government joined forces in the 20th century. Many clues lie in the carvings on Tikal's hardwood lintels, which, hidden from the sun beneath palace ceilings, are well preserved.

More than 3,000 mapped structures, 250 stelae, and a surreal living jungle will keep visitors with sturdy walking shoes happy for days. Among the discoveries in Tikal, a calendar stone was found here with skull-and-bone imagery, and **Stela 29** bears the earliest Long Count date yet found in the Maya lowlands: A.D. 292, considered the official start of the Classic Period. The latest date is on **Stela 11,** carved in A.D. 869. In between, the stelae record the births and deaths of kings, the cycle of festivals and seasons, and the sagas of war, telling the epic story of a 1,000-year dynasty of 39 kings, each commemorated among the ruins. Yax Moch Xoc founded this dynasty, ruling A.D. 219–238. His descendants, the royalty of Tikal, include kings such as Great-Jaguar-Paw, Moon-Zero Bird, and Curl-Snout.

But it is Tikal's tallest structures—its soaring temples standing out of the forest canopy—that form its most enduring images. Tikal feels so otherworldly that director George Lucas used the view from Temple IV to portray a rebel base in *Star Wars: Episode IV* (on the Massassi Outpost, on the fourth moon of Yavin, if you must know).

The Ruins

The **Great Plaza** was the heart of ancient Tikal, complex in design and covering about three acres. Its plastered floor, now covered with grass, is made of four layers, the earliest laid in 150 B.C. and the latest in A.D. 700.

The great **Temple I** (The Great Jaguar) faces **Temple II** (Temple of the Masks) across the plaza. Temple I is 44 meters (144 feet) tall. This imposing structure is the tomb of Hasaw Chan K'awil (Heavenly Standard Bearer), the ruler who successfully led Tikal to victory against Calakmul. (The museum contains a reconstruction of the tomb.) Unfortunately, it is no longer possible to climb Temple I.

The slightly smaller Temple II was built to honor Hasaw Chan K'awil's wife, Lady 12 Macaw. Large, severely eroded masks flank the central staircase, while a staircase to the side allows access to the top.

The **East Plaza,** which backs up to the Temple of the Jaguar, was once a formal plastered area covering 5.5 acres. Two of the city's causeways, **Mendez** and **Maler,** lead from here. This plaza is the site of the only known sweathouse at Tikal; it's also the site of a **ball court** and what appears to be the marketplace.

Around the area, scattered palaces, altars, and over 70 stelae tell of Maya life and conquest. Most of these palaces were ceremonial centers, but a few are believed to have been apartments. If you climbed and poked around into every structure at the Great Plaza, it would take you at least an entire day.

It's a nice walk to **Temple IV** (Temple of the Double-Headed Serpent), and a trip to this iconic, steep building is a must. Facing east, it's a popular spot from which to watch the sunrise. The platform itself has not been excavated, and only those in good physical condition will want to climb the six ladders (sometimes all you can cling to are roots and branches) to the top. Yaxkin Caan Chac, the son and successor of Ah-Cacau, built Temple IV around A.D. 740, about 40 years after Temple I was built for his father. Today, Temple IV is the tallest surviving Maya structure from pre-Columbian history—212 feet from the base of its platform to the top. Not until the turn of the 20th century were taller buildings constructed in this hemisphere. Temple IV also houses a three-room

GUATEMALA

temple, with walls up to 40 feet thick. From the summit of Temple IV, the sight of the entire area is breathtaking. The jungle canopy itself rises 100 feet into the air, and the tops of the other temples of Tikal rise above the tops of the trees.

Though the climb to the top of Temple IV is strenuous, it pales in comparison to the ascent to the north-facing **Temple V**. Like Temple I, it was built about A.D. 700 and rises about 190 feet.

Visiting the Site

Tikal is open 6 A.M.–6 P.M. daily. If you arrive after 3 P.M., your ticket should be stamped with the next day's date, allowing you to enter the ruins the next day at no additional cost. Entrance costs US$19 (US$3 for Guatemalan nationals). Check the park's official website (www.tikalpark.com) for the latest rates and event announcements.

The main gate is on the road from El Remate, where there's a checkpoint. From here, it's another 17 kilometers (10.5 mi) to the main parking lot and visitors center. Tickets are checked at a booth on the trail between the visitors center and the entrance to the ruins proper, opposite an oft-photographed ceiba tree gracing the side of the road.

At the visitors center, there is a scale model of the site, two museums (the Stela Museum and the Morley Museum), an overpriced eatery, and a few small shops selling books, souvenirs, snacks, and sundries, including bug spray and sunscreen. Nearby is the park campsite, police substation, and a post office. You can book licensed guides at the visitors center (US$40 for up to four people, US$5 for each additional person). Be sure to pick up archaeologist William Coe's *Tikal: A Handbook of the Ancient Maya Ruins,* which has the best map of the site.

The ruins of Tikal sprawl over six square miles, connected by a fantastic, sometimes confusing trail system. This means you'll be doing a lot of walking, nearly all of it on flat ground—except, of course, when climbing the pyramids. Prepare as you would for a nature hike rather than a museum visit: comfortable walking shoes, a snack, more water than you think you'll need, and a rain jacket during the wet season (or for when the monkeys pee on you—seriously). There are a number of shelters in case it really starts coming down, and a few beverage stands, but no food is available.

There are plenty of accommodations in El Remate and Flores, but nothing beats staying right here in the park at one of four lodgings: **Jungle Lodge** (tel. 502/2476-8775, www.junglelodge.guate.com, US$40–80), **Jaguar Inn** (tel. 502/7926-0002, www.jaguartikal.com, US$65 d), **Tikal Inn** (hoteltikalinn@itelgua.com, US$60–100), and **Tikal Campground** (US$4 per person). Although you can hire a guide at the park entrance, you're probably better off going through a tour company in Flores or at your hotel. Bird-watchers especially will appreciate tours offered by **Hotel La Casa de Don David** (tel. 502/7928-8469 or 502/5306-2190, www.lacasadedondavid.com) in El Remate, which is celebrating 2012 with a lecture series and Maya Universe Garden around a sacred ceiba tree.

In 2012

On October 21, 2012, Tikal will host celebrations for the **Día de La Raza** (Day of the Races), an alternative to Columbus Day, which celebrates the accomplishments of the Latin American people and honors indigenous cultures. Expect a Maya event and ceremony to take place at Tikal on December 21.

Getting There

Flores is a popular airport for Tikal visitors from Belize City or Guatemala City, and it has a relatively modern small terminal. Tikal is three hours or less from the Belize border at **Melchor,** and it is a popular day trip for travelers in Belize. Other travelers base themselves in Flores and El Remate, where transportation to and from the ruins is part of daily life. Of course signing up for a day trip to Tikal from either Flores, El Remate, or the Cayo District in Belize is also a possibility. Transportation is available in any of those towns to make it there on your own.

UAXACTÚN

Uaxactún is a Middle Preclassic site dating to about 600 B.C. that came into its own in the Late Preclassic sometime between 350 B.C. and A.D. 250. Sylvanus G. Morley rediscovered Uaxactún in 1916. Its original name has subsequently been deciphered as Siaan K'aan ("Born in Heaven"), though Morley supposedly chose the name Uaxatún ("Eight Stone") as a reference to a stone dating to the 8th *b'aktun,* then the earliest-known date inscription. Some believe his choice of name was a nod to "Washington," the U.S. capital and home of the Carnegie Institute that funded his explorations.

The ruins are smaller than Tikal and not as well preserved. Uaxactún's most distinct structure is its **observatory,** believed to be one of the first astronomical complexes and aligned with the equinoxes and the solstices.

A 15-minute walk southeast of the airstrip leads to **Group E,** a series of small, partially restored temples arranged side by side, oriented north to south, and designed as an astronomical observatory. They align with the sunrise on key dates. When viewed from the top of nearby **Temple E-VII-Sub,** the sun rises over E-1 on the summer solstice and over the southernmost E-III on the winter solstice. Temple E-VII-Sub's foundations date to 2,000 B.C.

Visiting the Site

Uaxactún lies at the end of an unpaved road, which is usually passable by 4WD vehicle—usually. The site is very remote; there are no set hours, no entrance fee, and very few services.

There are several primitive lodging and dining options in Uaxactún, which form a tiny remote forest community. The best accommodations are at **Campamento El Chiclero** (tel. 7926-1095, US$7 per person) on the north end of the airstrip. You can also camp or string a hammock (US$3) here. An on-site restaurant ($5 per meal) serves large portions of good, basic food. The friendly owners can arrange trips to some of the more remote places in the biosphere reserve. **Aldana's Lodge** is just off the street leading to Groups A and B with

© AL ARGUETA

GUATEMALA

Petén forest at Uaxactún: the setting for important equinox and solstice ceremonies

simple *palapa*-roof cabanas (US$4 per person, camping US$2 per person). Aldana's can also arrange visits to area sites.

Eat at your choice of three simple *comedores* in town.

In 2012

Spring and fall equinox are a big deal at Uaxactún, even more so in 2012. Expect ceremonies and sunrise vigils at the ancient observatory of Group E. There, three small temples arranged in a triangle will perfectly frame the rising sun on the spring (Mar. 22) and fall (Sept. 21) equinoxes, as well as for a few days before and after. The equinox will be marked by sunrise ceremonies over three days led by learned Maya "counters of the days," or *tatas* (male spiritual leaders) and *nanas* (female spiritual leaders). Nearly a dozen of these spiritual leaders will come together to welcome the birth of the sun with music, dancing, sacred fires, and chanting. Specially trained athletes will demonstrate the Maya ball game and there will be performances by local dance troupes, as well as cheap cold beer in the evening at the one local bar. Arrange a homestay for a true cultural immersion.

A one-time 30Q entry fee (US$4) will be charged to enter the village during the equinox celebrations. Contact the **Turismo de Arqueología** (tel. 502/7926-4068, turismo-comunitariouaxactun@yahoo.com) for information about shuttle van transportation from Tikal to Uaxactún and to reserve a homestay or camping spot (25Q per person or US$4).

Getting There

Visits to Uaxactún begin in **Flores** or **El Remate,** as do those for Tikal. A bus leaves Santa Elena at 1 P.M. daily, stopping in Tikal at about 3 P.M. From there it's about 1.5 hours to Uaxactún. These times are very flexible. By car, be aware that the road is passable only in a 4WD vehicle at any time of year. If you're unable to fill your gas tank in Flores, the last gas station en route is at Ixlú, south of El Remate.

YAXHÁ

Yaxhá is one of those barely visited sites that travelers have been whispering about for years. It was a small city, southeast of Tikal, and gets about a thousand times fewer visitors. The site is only partially excavated and restored as part of an ongoing German-Guatemalan partnership.

Yaxhá's buildings were constructed with a lighter-colored limestone than found at other sites, giving it a unique aesthetic, especially contrasted against the dark greenery. The ruins are spread over nine plazas containing 500 mapped structures including temples, ball courts, and palaces.

Begin with the sweet vista from **Structure 216,** atop a wooden staircase built into the temple's side. Other highlights include the recently restored **North Acropolis,** surrounded by three temples, two of which are fairly large. A path known as **Calzada Blom** leads almost one kilometer north from here to the **Maler**

Group, a complex featuring twin temples facing each other across a plaza similar to the setup at Tikal. A number of weathered **stelae** and the broken remains of a large circular altar further adorn the complex. Another great location affording wonderful views closer to the heart of the ruined city is the top of an unnamed **astronomical observation pyramid** between Plaza F and Structure 116.

Visiting the Site

Yaxhá is open 8 A.M.–5 P.M. daily. Entrance costs US$10. A parking lot and restrooms are on the east side of the park, as is a small museum. There are two boat docks, one below the parking lot and one at the western end of the site.

You can camp for free at **Campamento Yaxhá,** a designated lakeside campsite below the ruins proper. **Reserva Natural Privada Yaxhá** (tel. 502/2366-3411, www.yaxhanatural.org) is a private 407-hectare nature reserve and the site of a biological field station with dorms for up to 20 people. The reserve is most easily accessible by boat from the Yaxhá archaeological site.

Getting There

Yaxhá is located 31 kilometers (19 mi) east of **Ixlú,** off the road toward the Belize border. A well-marked turnoff leads a further 11 kilometers (7 mi) north to the Yaxhá guardpost, where you pay admission and sign in to the park. From there, it's another three kilometers (2 mi) to the actual ruins of Yaxhá. The road is in good condition, even during the rainy season.

If traveling by bus, get off at the junction to Yaxhá and hitch a ride with an occasional passing pickup truck or fellow travelers. (There is some traffic along this route because of the presence of the small village of La Máquina, about two kilometers, or 1.2 miles from the park guard post.) Several Belize and Flores tour operators offer day trips to Yaxhá.

QUIRIGUÁ

Quiriguá is a Classic era site on the Guatemalan side of the Río Motagua. It has a history closely intertwined with that of Copán, 30 miles due south in Honduras. In 1981, Quiriguá was given UNESCO World Heritage Site status. The site itself is located between Guatemala City and the Caribbean coast at Puerto Barrios and is surrounded by vast expanses of banana plantations.

Quiriguá has some of the largest carved Maya stelae ever found, including a 65-ton mammoth known as **Stela E**. This stela is 35 feet tall (and eight feet underground) and dates to A.D. 771. This was during the illustrious, eventful rule of Cauac Sky, who rebelled against Copán, to which Quiriguá had been subservient for centuries. Things ended after Copán's king, 18 Rabbit, lost his head after a ritual ball game. Thus began Quiriguá's reign of the area until A.D. 810, the city's last recorded date.

Local sandstone allowed Quiriguá's artists to make particularly intricate carvings and Long Count dates. On altar **Zoomorph O**, for example, there is a *k'atun* ending of 9.18.0.0.0 (October 11, A.D. 790) next to a dancing glyph of Chaac the rain god. In fact, Quiriguá's inscriptions are considered to be some of the finest glyph work in the Mundo Maya. Many of the best stelae are protected under simple thatch structures in the **Great Plaza** and near the **Acropolis**.

Visiting the Site

Quiriguá is open 7:30 A.M.–5 P.M. daily. Entrance costs US$5. A few food stands, a ticket office, and a small museum mark the entrance. There is a small model that gives a sense of what has been excavated and what remains hidden. The nearest accommodations are in Los Amates, at Km. 200 of Highway CA-9.

Getting There

Quiriguá is located four kilometers (2.5 mi) off Highway CA-9 (at Km. 204), the main road from **Guatemala City** toward Puerto Barrios. This makes it a natural stopover for anyone traveling between these two sites, and it is very accessible by car or bus.

PIEDRAS NEGRAS

Piedras Negras lies on a wide bank of the Río Usumacinta, the longest river in Central America. It is about as far away in the Mesoamerican wild as you can possibly be—surrounded on all sides by the thick forests of the Sierra del Lacandón, with barely a road in sight. Piedras Negras was founded around A.D. 300 and fought with Yaxchilán (40 km upstream on the Mexico side) over control of the river route for much of its history.

Today, Piedras Negras is threatened by the proposal to build a hydroelectric dam some 30 miles downstream on the Río Usumacinta at Boca de Cerro. If this happens, 18 archaeological sites would be lost underwater.

Archaeologists have uncovered eight **sweat baths,** with fire hearths lined with potsherds, benches, and floors equipped with drains. The remains of Russian Maya scholar Tatiana Proskouriakoff (1909–1985), who studied Piedras Negras extensively, are buried under the floor of Structure J-23 in the **Acropolis** (a twin-palace) near Group F. Many fine **stelae** were placed before the temples here, and a few of Piedras Negras's inscriptions mention future cycle endings.

Visiting the Site

Piedras Negras is very remote; there are no set hours and entrance is free. The easiest way to visit the site is to sign up with a tour that specializes in trips here, like **Maya Expeditions** (www.mayaexpeditions.com), or through the **Posada Maya** (tel. 502/7861-1799, US$20) in Bethel. There is a riverside campsite on a sandy beach just a few hundred meters downstream from Piedras Negras; bring your own gear. In Bethel, you can book a guided overnight camping trip to the ruins and river (US$125).

Getting There

This is one of the most remote Maya sites in the entire Mundo Maya, on the far western panhandle of the Petén, so getting there is part of the experience. Only about 200 tourists make the trip annually, so don't expect crowds. Access is from **Bethel** or **Frontera Corozal.** Visitors then head downstream by boat to Piedras Negras, which is beyond Yaxchilán.

TAK'ALIK AB'AJ

Tak'alik Ab'aj, the "place of standing stones," is located in southwestern Guatemala, near the Pacific Coast and the border with Mexico in the municipality of El Asintal, department of Retalhuleu. The site was a commercial and political center from 800 B.C. to A.D. 200, and lays in a low, damp zone that was a major center for growing cacao. Cacao and salt were traded for obsidian, quetzal feathers, pyrite, and jade. (Today, farmers have switched mostly to coffee.)

For archaeologists, Tak'alik Ab'aj has emerged as an important Preclassic site that speaks of the transition from pre-Maya to Maya. It has definite evidence of an Olmec invasion, including samples of pot-bellied *barrigones* ceramic figures, Olmecoid heads, and a distinct Olmec monument.

The nearly 300 excavated monuments and structures at Tak'alik Ab'aj comprise 80 buildings constructed around a dozen plazas. The site covers an area of about 2.5 square miles and features river-rock temple facades atop nine terraces sculpted from the hillside. **Structure 5** is the tallest temple, with a 16-meter-high vantage of the city. **Structure 7** may have served as an astronomical observatory.

Discoveries continue at this site. In 2004, archaeologists discovered the **tomb** of Tak'alik Ab'aj's last ruler, which dated to about A.D. 100. In 2010, an exquisite jade head was found.

Several Long Count *b'aktun* dates have been recorded here, specifically *b'aktun* 7 and 8 carved into several **stelae.** The recently discovered **Monument 48** is believed to mirror the iconography at Izapa of "the solar deity or lord enthroned in the belly of the Milky Way," states John Major Jenkins. The iconography "represents the birth of the sun on several different temporal levels—the new year at the December solstice—and a larger rebirth of the December solstice sun (specifically, in reference to the 13-Baktun World Age cycle in the Long Count calendar)."

Visiting the Site

Tak'alik Ab'aj is open 7 A.M.–5 P.M. daily. Entrance costs US$3.50. The **Takalik Maya Lodge** (tel. 502/2333-7056 or 502/2337-0037, www.takalik.com, US$80) is two kilometers (1.2 mi) up the road from the entrance.

Getting There

Tak'alik Ab'aj is located at Km. 199 on the Carretera al Pacífico (Pacific Coast Highway, CA-2). The closest town is **El Asintal,** five kilometers (3 mi) north of the highway; the turnoff is found at Km. 190.5. From the town of **Retalhuleu,** drive or take the bus to El Asintal. From El Asintal, pickup trucks will take you the remaining four kilometers (2.5 mi) to Tak'alik Ab'aj. Or take a taxi from Retalhuleu (US$30 round-trip).

Tours and Packages

CONFERENCES

Organized each year in March since 1977 by the University of Texas at Austin's Department of Art and Art History, **The Maya Meetings** (www.utmaya.org) is an academic conference that "draws scholars from a wide spectrum of relevant fields, as well as interested non-professionals, to interact creatively and share the most recent insights on Maya and Mesoamerican research." In 2011, the conference's theme was "2012: Time and Prophecy in the Mesoamerican World." The 2012 event will take place in Antigua, Guatemala, March 12–17. Some of the bigger names in Maya studies and 2012ology will be present.

COMMUNITY TOURISM

A medical congress related to 2012 with **Adrenalina Tours** (www.adrenalinatours.com), a tour operator based in Quetzaltenango, will focus on sustainable tourism.

GUATEMALA

© JOSHUA BERMAN

The author entertains local youth during a community project in northern Guatemala.

Huehuetenango Community Ecological Tourism Project

I have been told that Huehuetenango is the up-and-coming spot for grassroots village-based tourism, especially since a recent investment by the European Union built basic infrastructure and provided training to get the project off the ground. To explore this completely untapped region of western Guatemala and support a worthy venture, visit the Huehuetenango Community Ecological Tourism Project (www.todossantoscuchumatan.weebly.com or www.laantesaladelcielo.blogspot.com) for a list of participating villages, prices for guesthouses and guides, and descriptions of local attractions. These community tourism projects are the first of their kind in these predominantly Mam Maya areas, and are visited by just a handful of visitors each year.

One option is **Lago Magdalena** (US$20 per person per day, includes guide), just above Lake Magdalena. Guests stay in one of six cabanas, made of river stone and wood, with electricity and shared outdoor toilets. Meals are arranged separately with a local cook.

La Ventosa and **Chiabal** (contact Esteban Matías, tel. 502/5381-0540, www.turismocuchumatanes.com, US$35 per person per day, includes lodging, guide, and three meals) are located about 45 minutes before Todos Santos. (Look for a collection of cabanas at nearly 11,000 feet on a wide, sheep-speckled plateau.) From here, you can climb El Torre, the highest non-volcanic peak in Central America.

Maya Foundations

Guatemala's poverty and human rights abuse history has ensured a large number of nonprofit organizations doing different work around the country. **Guatemala NGO Network** (www.laantiguaguatemala.net) is one site that consolidates and organizes various projects in the country. You can also do a "Guatemala" search at www.volunteerabroad.com. They usually have an overflowing database of extended travel opportunities.

The Antigua-based organization **Starfish**

Q&A: GASPAR PEDRO GONZÁLEZ, AUTHOR

As the allure of 2012 and its myriad meanings sweeps the globe, the Maya voice is often left out – but not always. Gaspar Pedro González was born and raised in a Q'anjobal Maya village high in the Cuchumatan Mountains, in the department of Huehuetenango. He is a novelist, philosopher, and professor at the esteemed University Mariano Gálvez, and a member of the Guatemalan Academy of Mayan Languages. His latest book, 13 B'aktun: Mayan Visions of 2012 and Beyond, is unlike any other on the subject, discussing 2012 in a deep, lyrical dialogue between child and elder. "In this book," he told me, "my hope is to inspire optimism about the new age; it should inspire hope, it should inspire a new dawn."

Why is 2012 a good year to visit the Mundo Maya?

With the ending of one of the longest Maya calendar cycles, visitors will have the opportunity to meet actual Maya, see their customs, their traditions, their form of life, and learn about their mysticism and philosophy. Most Maya are not in the capital; they're out in the villages and communities. But more than anything, people can learn about Maya values, which coincide with 2012, a time when we are asking human beings to be more conscious about humanity.

So Maya culture has a lot to contribute to the world, and to human beings in any part of the world. The Maya vision should be shared with other cultures. Ours is a vision toward the inside, not toward the outside; not to pursue riches and material things but to focus on the conservation of life and human values like justice, peace, and solidarity that will benefit the world.

What advice do you have for someone traveling to a Maya village or archaeological site for the first time?

First, they should seek out the ancient places and archaeological sites, and get information from living Maya about the meaning of each of the structures, their significance, and their view of the universe. It is important to understand the past to know the present times we are in, and also for looking forward as a whole humanity. There are beautiful geographical destinations in Guatemala, Chiapas, and Belize, and in addition to these natural places, there is a beautiful aesthetic in the way of life – in the traditional dress and oral traditions – that tourists should know, at least those tourists who would like to expand their vision of the world.

What does "responsible tourism" mean when traveling in the Mundo Maya?

It's important to look at two things: First, there is the traditional tourism through travel agencies, through the established infrastructure, and generally, in these countries of Mesoamerica, the infrastructure is not in Maya hands. It is in white people's hands; the Ladinos, they benefit more from tourism economically.

But if foreigners want to visit the more remote villages, to visit this essence of the culture, this essence of life, they should go to the smallest villages where they have conserved

One by One (www.starfishonebyone.org) works to educate girls and empower women in Maya communities surrounding Lake Atitlán. Starfish occasionally has volunteer opportunities.

The **Rigoberta Menchú Tum Foundation** (tel. 502/2230-2431 or 2232-0793, guatemala@frmt.org, www.frmt.org) considers itself "guardians of our territories which have the vastest biological diversity in the world." They offer various educational, development, and human rights related programs in which you can become involved or support financially.

MayaWorks (tel. 312/243-8050, info@ mayaworks.org, www.mayaworks.org) is a nonprofit organization that helps Maya women start small businesses and sell fair-trade crafts. They partner with 125 artisans in the central highlands of Guatemala. You can support them right now by shopping, donating, or

COURTESY OF GASPAR PEDRO GONZÁLEZ

Gaspar Pedro González is considered to be the first Maya novelist.

the Mayan languages and form of life. Surely the Maya will benefit from this tourism. The tourist wants to see new things even though maybe in the smaller pueblos, there aren't as many comforts, only simple *pensiones*, but that is where you'll find the essence of life and the essence of the culture.

The Maya understand that there are differences between our culture and the cultures of different parts of the world. Nobody should be afraid to come to Guatemala as a tourist because there is brotherhood, solidarity, and the Maya, in general, are very hospitable. For the Maya it is an honor to have a foreigner in their home, so don't feel like it's a problem or a chore or an inconvenience or an invasion of their home, no. Hospitality is an important value that we practice.

volunteering on their website. In 2012, they're offering a tour (10 days, Feb. 17–26, US$1,450) where travelers can visit some of the artisans and learn about their lives and villages.

TOURS IN 2012

There should be hundreds of events around the country and throughout the year. Independent travelers with a nose for these things can easily just show up and follow their whims. Or, you can put your itinerary in someone else's hands and sign up to one of the following tours, each one approaching the 2012 theme with their own Guatemala perspective.

Aventuras en Educación

Aventuras en Educación (www.adventurestudy. com or www.losencuentros.com), in collaboration with Hotel San Buenaventura in Antigua, is offering a weeklong **Dawn of a New Age** tour (7 days, July 6–13, Nov. 7–16, Dec. 14–21, US$512–722 per person double occupancy) in Lake Atitlán. Richard Morgan Szybist, resident expert and author of several books on the lake basin and its culture, leads the tours and considers Lake Atitlán "one of the planet's energy vortexes." The tour is based in the lakeside town of Panajachel, which has basic services like restaurants, banking, and Internet access. Many activities will be conducted on the grounds of Hotel San Buenaventura, which is surrounded by a coffee plantation and nature reserve. Expect regional Maya cuisine, a fire ceremony, a personal Maya spiritual cleansing treatment, and a reading of your birth date based on Maya calendar energies.

Aventuras en Educación also offers a **Land of the Living Maya** tour (US$910–1,534 per person) with 10- and 16-day extensions into Petén. Tours cover some of the sites listed above, and include visits to the ruins of the Kaqchikel Maya, one of the two Maya peoples who still populate Atitlán. Meet indigenous *arte naïf* painters, weavers who dye their own thread from plants grown around the lake, and healers who cure with traditional medicinal plants.

Mayan Zone

Mayan Zone (tel. 502/2364-8456 or 502/4024-8979, infoguate@mayan-zone.com, www.mayan-zone.com) is a Guatemala-based tour operator with experience throughout the Maya region. Tours are focused on travelers who enjoy mixing with the local population and learning about indigenous customs and life in Guatemala. The eight-day **Discovery of the Altiplano and the Ixil Triangle** is available year-round (outside peak seasons). The trip starts in Antigua and continues with a full tour of the Lake Atitlán area including Chichicastenango, Acul, Chajul, Nebaj, and Iximché. This is an active, thorough tour, and you'll meet all kinds of people—from village artisans to the Department Chief of Sacred Sites for the Ministry of Culture, who is also a Maya priest and calendar keeper.

If that's not enough, go with the whole enchilada: the **Guatemala, A Sacred Land–2012** tour. This is a 15-day feast of deep Mundo Maya travel, beginning in Antigua and including homestays in nearby Cakchiquel and Tz'utujil Maya villages. You'll spend days touring the lake (often by boat) and visiting villages such as San Juan la Laguna, a Tzutujil community on the lake's edge. Attend weaving workshops with local women, hit the highlands, visit Iximché archaeological site, and visit Maximon, a local saint venerated by a Christian-Maya cult in Santiago. The trip includes long excursions through the Petén and Copán, Honduras.

MayaSites Travel

MayaSites Travel (tel. 877/620-8715, mayasites@yahoo.com, www.mayasites.com) is offering a **Birthplace of the Maya Long Count Calendar: Western Guatemala Highlands** tour (6 nights, Dec. 17–23, US$1,780 per person double occupancy) entirely in Guatemala, flying in and out of Guatemala City. The tour focuses on modern Maya culture and archaeological sites with the earliest Long Count calendar dates ever discovered. This includes Tak'alik Ab'aj, Ixmiche, Santiago de Atitlán, Chichicastenango, Quetzaltenango, Antigua, and Izapa (Mexico), plus a gala dinner with a 2012 countdown and special talks on the Maya calendar.

Robert Roskind and Tata Pedro Cruz

The authors of the book *2012: The Transformation from the Love of Power to the Power of Love* will host several spiritual adventures in the Guatemalan highlands. Trips will teach that the end of the 2012 cycle will "restore a vibration of love to the planet and should not be feared but welcomed." For the winter solstice, they will host a Guatemala Gathering of the Peacemakers (Dec. 17–23) at Lake Atitlán.

Unificación Maya

Unificación Maya (www.ixcanaan.com) is a program offered in December 2011 and December 2012. (They've been doing it for six years, leading up to the 2012 event.) The trip is based at Hotel Gringo Perdido (www.hotelgringoperdido.com) in El Remate and offers **7 Sacred Mayan Fire Ceremonies in 7 Sacred Sites over 7 Days** with the goal "to bring together a great number of like-minded people, gathering finally in the Central Plaza of Tikal at the winter solstice, the time of rebirth." Along the way, you'll learn your Maya birth glyph, participate in ceremonies, visit the archaeological sites of Petén, sample local food and drink, learn Mayan phrases and cosmology, and meet the *tatas* and *nanas* of present-day Maya.

Villa Sumaya

Sign up for a yoga and personal growth retreat on the shores of Lake Atitlán at Villa Sumaya (retreatsatvillasumaya@yahoo.com, www.villasumaya.com), located in the town of Santa Cruz La Laguna. In 2012, Vincent Stanzione, an expert on Mesoamerican culture and the head of Villa Sumaya's Mayan Studies Project, will offer lectures on "Introduction to Mayan Day-Keeping," "The Mayan Calendar," and "Two Calendars in One: the Solar Round." If you are in the area, Stanzione is also available as a Maya storyteller for groups of four people or more.

Chocolate Tours

Cultural Crossroads (tel. 802/479-7040, www.culturalcrossroads.com), a Vermont-based tour operator, is offering the eight-day trip From Plant to Palate: Coffee and Chocolate in Guatemala (Feb. 12–19, US$3,525 per person), based in Antigua. Trips to Maya ruins are mixed with a full-immersion coffee and cacao experience—from hands-on classes to market visits and discussions about fair trade. You'll meet people in the trade including farmers, roasters, weavers, and chefs. A wine and chocolate reception is held by the Director of the Museum of Modern Art in Guatemala City before a private tour of the museum. Opt for the extension to Copán, Honduras, and attend a cacao seminar at a 100-year-old converted farmhouse, with a full tour of local Maya culture and the archaeological site.

If you find yourself in *el barrio historico* in Quetzaltenango, Guatemala, and you'd like to know what fifth-generation artisan chocolate tastes like, give a call to **Chocolate Doña Pancha** (10a Calle 16-67 zona 1, tel. 502/7761-9700, www.chocolatedonapancha.com) for a tour of the facility and to see their display on cacao and what it means to the Maya. Run by a 100 percent Quezalteca family who is very proud of their tradition and happy to offer you a taste.

HOTEL PACKAGES

Posada Belen (tel. 866/864-8283, www.guatemaya.com) will be offering a modification of their **Guatemala Classic Journey** (9 days, US$899 double occupancy) in Tikal, including a ceremony on December 21, 2012.

Eco Hotel Uxlabil Atitlán (San Juan la Laguna Sololá, tel. 502/2366-9555, www.atitlan.uxlabil.com) is run by Francisco Sandoval, a cultural anthropologist who plans to crank up the frequency of their *tuj,* a ritual Maya sauna, in 2012.

GUATEMALA

BELIZE

There I was, chest-deep in the Maya underworld, the sounds of slapping water echoing through the cave. My headlamp washed through the crystal-clear underground river, revealing tiny fish trying to nibble at my knees. I was in Actun Tunichil Muknal, the "Cave of the Crystal Maiden" and one of the most mind-blowing adventures that anyone (older than 12 and in good shape) can experience.

I was there in good company, tromping into the earth with Belize's top archaeologist, Dr. Jaime Awe, a Travel Channel film crew, and 17 porters and guides floating and lugging several 1,000 pounds of lights and batteries through the cave's many turns. It felt like an expedition worthy of the site.

Finally, we emerged from the water, removed our shoes, and sock-padded up the clay, past

hundreds—thousands—of potsherds and human skull fragments. As the film crew's powerful lights clicked on in the cathedral room, I watched as everyone was stunned into silence—even Dr. Awe, who had been here many times before, but had never seen it lit up so beautifully. He pointed to the bones of several infant sacrifices, then the crystal maiden herself, lying right where she had fallen as an offering to Chaac, the rain god. This was the evidence behind Dr. Awe's latest work, which pointed to severe droughts that pushed the Maya to offer younger, more precious lives to the gods—and to do it deeper and deeper inside Xibalba, the sacred underworld.

Dr. Awe pointed to some ash on the ground and told me that where we were standing, over a thousand years ago, a group of Maya had

© JOSHUA BERMAN

BELIZE

To Tulum

MEXICO

Corozal Town
SANTA RITA
AVENTURA
CERRO MAYA
NOHMUL
COROZAL DISTRICT
SAN ANTONIO RÍO HONDA
SHIPSTERN
Orange Walk Town
Ambergris Caye
CUELLO
San Pedro
EL POSITO

Río Hondo

ORANGE WALK DISTRICT
LAS MILPAS
LAMANAI
ALTUN HA
EL INFIERNO
KAKABISH
CHAN CHICH
SAN JOSE
BELIZE DISTRICT
Belize City

BELIZE

Northern Two Caye
Turneffe Islands

EL PILAR
BARTON RAMIE
BELMOPAN
XUNANTUNICH
San Ignacio
ACTÚN TUNICHIL MUKNAL
CAHAL PECH
To Tikal
TIPU
MUCNAL TUNICH
CAYO DISTRICT
POMONA
Dangriga
KUCHIL BALUM
KENDAL
TZIMIN KAX
Maya Center
Glover's Reef
CARACOL
STANN CREEK DISTRICT
ACTUN BALAM
RED BANK
TOLEDO DISTRICT
Placencia

Caribbean Sea

NIM LI PUNIT
XNAHEB
LUBAANTUN
San Pedro Columbia
UXBENKA
PUSILHA
HOKEB HA
Punta Gorda

Gulf of Honduras

GUATEMALA

0 30 mi
0 30 km

BELIZE

© AVALON TRAVEL

tamped their torches against the cave wall. It looked like fresh cigar ash. I got the chills.

The cave felt delicate, but it was no accident or oversight that allowed tourists to trounce through such a rare preserve. It was, in fact, a strategy to preserve the site. Dr. Awe explained that training local tour guides gave them a stake in the business of showing the cave and its contents to visitors. They then become stewards and protectors of the place.

My trip to the Belizean underworld reflects the rest of my experience traveling in Belize: surprising, awe-inspiring, cool, and deep—at least up to your chest.

HISTORY

Evidence of pre-Maya Archaic peoples in northern Belize indicates habitation at least 10,000 years ago. Later Belize developed Preclassic and Classic societies, which were part of a loose empire of city-states extending into present-day Guatemala, Mexico, and Honduras. One of its sites, Lamanai, remained occupied by Maya all the way up until contact with the Spanish. This happened relatively late in the 16th century, because the Spanish left the backwater of Belize alone for the most part.

After the Classic collapse around A.D. 900, it is unclear where many of Belize's original Maya went. Eventually, different groups migrated back to Belize to escape persecution elsewhere. Many of Belize's northern Maya came to escape the Yucatán Caste War, beginning around 1850. Thousands of Maya, mestizo, and Mexican refugees entered Belize to escape the widespread violence in Quintana Roo. These Yucatecans introduced Latin culture, Catholic religion, and agriculture into northern Belize, locally referred to as "Spanish tradition."

But even with the recent resurgence of Maya pride, the Maya of Belize are still among the poorest, most politically marginalized people in the country, especially in the southern Toledo District, where rural poverty and government neglect among the predominantly Mopan and Qéqchi' Maya villages is widespread. Most of these Maya are relatively recent immigrants as well. Escaping violence and repression in Guatemala over the last few generations, these informal, undocumented immigrants entered southern Belize and began working and living on the land.

PLANNING YOUR TIME

Most Maya-centered Belize trips are based in San Ignacio or Punta Gorda. **San Ignacio** (aka Cayo) is a riverside town in the western Cayo District with its own ancient Maya palace, Cahal Pech, at the highest point in town. You'll find the greatest density of archaeological sites in Cayo District, including **Xunantunich**, the site of the country's biggest event on December 21, 2012. The area is also home to **Caracol**, an important Classic Period city, and sacred ceremonial caves full of relics and bones. Stay at a guesthouse in San Ignacio, or head to one of the numerous remarkable jungle lodges in the area.

The Toledo Ecotourism Association is south, based in the Maya villages of the Toledo District. Here you'll find the unique archaeological sites of **Lubaantun** and **Nim Li Punit**. A trip here begins in **Punta Gorda** (called "PG"), a seaside village easily accessible by a domestic flight from Belize City (or a six-hour bus ride). Participants in the guesthouse program should plan on a few nights in one of the upcountry villages, plus a night in Punta Gorda on either end.

Ocean lovers should plan a side trip to **Corozal**, where Cerros (or Maya Hill) archaeological site overlooks the peaceful bay. You'll find some interesting Maya history at the Bacalar Chico Marine Reserve on the north tip of Ambergris Caye as well.

In 2012

From the image of Altun Ha's main temple on your bottle of Belikin beer to the surge of Maya-related events planned in Belize in 2012, the Maya spirit is very much alive here, where Mopan, Yucatec, and Q'eqchi' Maya have small communities across the country.

When it comes to planning ahead and promoting "The Year of the Maya," Belize is, by far, the most organized, forward-thinking country in the region. The Belize Tourism Board (www.travelbelize.org) has an official 2012 slogan, phrased as a challenge: "Where will you be when the world begins anew?" A detailed, constantly updated listing of events, conferences, races, concerts, and festivals is posted on their website.

As part of the broader 2012 campaign, the Belize Tourism Board is offering a special **2012 Passport,** which allows travelers to purchase bulk visits to the main archaeological sites; it includes a special commemorative book, stamps, cards, and stickers to collect at each site. These should be available at hotels and airports.

Maya Archaeological Sites

Archaeologists estimate that at one time, as many as two million Maya may have lived in what is now Belize. Belize has dozens of accessible, lushly vegetated archaeological sites, some fully excavated and restored, others barely peeking through centuries of ferns, trees, and monkeys. New sites are discovered each year in Belize, and it's common for rural families to have small ruins and mounds in their backyards.

The Belize Institute of Archaeology manages all archaeological sites as part of the government's **National Institute of Culture and History** (NICH, www.nichbelize.org). The following sites are listed as they appear from north Belize (near Corozal and Orange Walk), west (Cayo District), and then south (Toledo District).

Belize's Maya sites are not known for Long Count calendar inscriptions nor direct references to 2012 (not yet, anyway—discoveries are made constantly), but they are stunning and unique in different ways, and many will be hosting equinox and solstice ceremonies throughout 2012.

Belize's archaeological sites—both above- and belowground—are as impressive and varied as anywhere else in the Maya world, and though living Maya only comprise about 10 percent of Belize's already small population, the culture and physical ruins are things with which most Belizeans feel a connection—especially when there's a party involved, which there are sure to be plenty of in 2012.

CERRO MAYA

On the coast of northern Belize, Cerros, or Cerro Maya ("Maya Hill") as it is officially called, lies on a peninsula called Lawry's Bite. It is across Corozal Bay from the tranquil little port town of Corozal, a stone's throw from Mexico.

Cerros archaeological site is a principal attraction for travelers staying in Corozal town, near the border. The ruins of Cerros rise over sea and forest. The place served as an important coastal trading center during the Late Preclassic Period (350 B.C.–A.D. 250) and was occupied as late as A.D. 1300. Magnificent **frescoes** and stone heads were uncovered by archaeologist David Friedel, signifying that elite rule was firmly fixed by the end of the Preclassic Period. The tallest of Cerros's **temples** rises 70 feet, and because of the rise in the sea level, the onetime stone residences of the elite Maya are partially flooded.

It would appear that Cerros not only provisioned oceangoing canoes, but also was in an ideal location to control ancient trade routes that traced the Río Hondo and New River from the Yucatán to Petén and the Usumacinta basin. A plaster-lined canal for the sturdy, oversized ocean canoes was constructed around Cerros. Archaeologists have determined that extensive fishing and farming on raised fields took place, probably to outfit the traders.

Visiting the Site

Cerro Maya is open 8 A.M.–5 P.M. daily. Entrance costs US$5 per person. Be prepared for vicious mosquitoes at Cerros, depending on the time of year—especially if there is no breeze.

In 2012

A cycling race, the **Pablo Marin Classic,** and associated festivals and events are planned for

BELIZE

BELIZE

Q&A: KAREN CATCHPOLE AND ERIC MOHL, TRAVEL JOURNALISTS

In April 2006, journalist Karen Catchpole and photographer Eric Mohl left New York City in a pickup truck and embarked on their Trans-Americas Journey: a multi-year, 200,000-mile working road trip through North, Central, and South America. Their itinerary has allowed them to move slowly and thoroughly southward. As they travel, they freelance for U.S. and Canadian magazines and newspapers. The couple have visited more than 50 archaeological sites throughout Mexico, Belize, and Guatemala and blog about their travels at www.trans-americas.com.

When did you first travel to a country in the Mundo Maya? Where did you go and how did it impact you?

The first Maya site we visited on our Trans-Americas Journey was a way-off-the-beaten-path gem called La Milpa in the Río Bravo Conservation Area in northern Belize. Believed to have been settled in 400 B.C., La Milpa is a wonderful example of the charms of a largely unexcavated site. Though archaeology professors and students from the United States have heavily studied La Milpa, its structures have not been unearthed or rebuilt in any way. What you see is what you get, including some fantastic stelae still in their original positions. But mostly what you see are rocky mounds which the jungle has long since reclaimed. Wandering amongst them your imagination goes wild picturing how the place might have looked when it was a thriving city. We think this sense of possibility and mystery is part of what hooks archaeologists.

What advice do you have for someone traveling to a Maya village or archaeological site for the first time?

Generally speaking, the Maya we've met are an easy-going, forgiving bunch, and they don't demand much beyond general good behavior. The best advice for behaving well in a Maya village applies to all cultures: Watch what the locals do and do the same. If no one wears shorts, don't wear shorts. If they don't touch each other when greeting or speaking, keep your hands to yourself. Smile. A lot. Speaking of smiles, many Maya don't mind having their pictures taken, but some do, and ALL of them will be happier if you learn how to say something like "You're beautiful! Can I take a picture?" in Spanish (which most Maya speak in addition to their own language).

What does "responsible tourism" mean when traveling in the Mundo Maya?

The problem with the phrase "responsible tourism" is that the word "responsible" means different things to different people. We try to employ a travel-version of "do unto others" whenever we are lucky enough to spend time in cultures other than our own where the rules might be unknown to us and our impact could be detrimental. All people on the planet want to be treated with respect and an open mind, and if you can keep both things handy your impact will be less detrimental and may even be positive.

What has been your most memorable travel moment so far traveling in the Mundo Maya?

The hot, multiday slog through the jungle to

October 12–14. The town will also sponsor trips to Cerros and Santa Rita.

Getting There

Cerros is reachable by boat from Corozal Town. Hire a boat from **Tony's Inn and Beach Resort** (tel. 501/422-2055 or 501/422-3555, www.tonysinn.com) in Corozal or check with a travel agent to arrange transportation. If you are traveling during the dry season (Jan.–Apr.), you can get to Cerros by car. The drive from Corozal takes up to 45 minutes, and you'll have to employ the hand-cranked Pueblo Nuevo Ferry. Guests at **Cerros Beach Resort** (tel. 501/623-9763 or 501/623-9530, www.cerrosbeachresort.com, US$40–60) can bike to the ruins; keep an eye out for jaguarundi, gray fox, and coatimundi along the way.

COURTESY OF KAREN CATCHPOLE AND ERIC MOHL

travel journalists Karen Catchpole and Eric Mohl at Altun Ha

reach El Mirador archaeological site [in Guatemala], one of the most remote and the most spectacular Mayan remains, is a physical challenge that produces the rush that comes with surviving the heat and the scorpions. Once there, your efforts are rewarded with time at a huge and extremely important site that is just the right mix of excavated and unexcavated. Because of its location, the site is rarely busy, which means you can climb to the top of the La Danta temple (one of the largest in the known Maya world) for sunrise or sunset and have the place (and the toucans, howler monkeys,

falcons, bats, and that setting or rising ball of fire) to yourself.

Do you have any travel plans in the year 2012?

If you can handle crowds, this is sure to be a special time at many of the main archaeological sites. Just don't expect to have the place to yourself! If crowds aren't your thing, head for any of the many, many lesser-known and less-visited sites like Uaxactún, north of Tikal. The celebrations there will be smaller, but the crowds will be too.

LAMANAI ARCHAEOLOGICAL ZONE

Lamanai is one of the largest and longest-inhabited ceremonial centers in Belize, an imperial port city encompassing ball courts, pyramids, and several exotic Maya features. It was still occupied when Europeans made contact. Hundreds of buildings have been identified in this two-square-mile area located

in thick jungle on the banks of the New River Lagoon.

Archaeologist David Pendergast headed a team from the Royal Ontario Museum that, after finding a number of children's bones buried under a stela, presumed human sacrifice was a part of the residents' religion. He also found large masks in several locations depicting a ruler wearing a crocodile headdress,

© JOSHUA BERMAN

park guide at Lamanai

hence the name Lamanai ("Submerged Crocodile").

The ruins of Lamanai huddle to one side of New River Lagoon and sprawl westward through the forest and under the village of Indian Church (a rural village that was relocated by the government from one part of the site to another in 1992). Excavations reveal continuous occupation and a high standard of living into the Postclassic Period. Lamanai is believed to have been occupied from 1500 B.C. to the 19th century—Spanish occupation is also apparent, with the remains of two Christian churches and a sugar mill built by British colonialists.

The landscape at most of Lamanai is forest; trees, vines, and strangler figs grow from the tops of buildings. The only sounds are birdcalls and howler monkeys' roars echoing off the stone temples.

The Ruins

The Lamanai archaeological site consists of four large temples, a residential complex, and a reproduction stela of a Maya elite, Lord Smoking Shell.

The Mask Temple N9-56 housed two significant tombs as well as two Early Classic stone masks. It was built around A.D. 450. The second mask on the temple was exposed in late 2010.

The High Temple N10-43 is 33 meters (100 feet) tall, the tallest securely dated Preclassic structure in the Maya area. The 360-degree view from above the canopy is remarkable.

Lamanai's **ball court** is smaller than those at other sites, leading some to speculate it was just symbolic. In 1980, archaeologists raised the huge stone disc marking the center of the court and found lidded vessels on top of a mercury puddle. Miniature vessels inside contained small jade and shell objects.

The **Royal Complex** was excavated in 2005. This was the residence of up to two dozen elite Lamanai citizens; you can see their beds, doorways, and the like.

The **Jaguar Temple N10-9** was dated to the 6th century but underwent structural modifications in the 8th and 13th centuries. Jade jewelry and a jade mask were discovered here, as was an animal-motif dish. Based on the animal remains and other evidence, archaeologists believe that this was the site of an enormous party and feast to celebrate the end of a drought in A.D. 950.

In 1983, archaeologists began an investigation of **The Stela Temple N10-27,** where they discovered a large stone monument. Designated Stela 9, it depicts Lord Smoking Shell in ceremonial dress. Hieroglyphic text of Stela 9, while incomplete, indicates that this monument was erected to commemorate the accession of Smoking Shell, the Lord of Lamanai. Today, a replica stands at the stela temple; the original can be viewed in the museum at Lamanai.

Wildlife and Bird-Watching

The trip up the New River Lagoon to the site is its own safari; once you're at the ruins, numbered trees correspond to an information pamphlet available from the caretakers at the entrance of Lamanai Reserve.

Bird-watchers, look around the **Mask Temple** and **High Temple** for Montezuma oropendola and their drooping nests. The black vulture is often spotted slowly gliding over the entire area. A woodpecker with a distinct double-tap rhythm and a red cap is the male pale-billed woodpecker. Near the High Temple, small flocks of collared aracaris, related to the larger toucan, forage the canopy for fruits and insects. The black-headed trogon is more spectacular than its name implies: a yellow chest, a black-and-white tail, and iridescent blue-green back. Though it looks as if the northern jacana is walking on water, it's the delicate floating vegetation that holds the long-toed bird above the water as it searches along the water's edge for edible delicacies.

Visiting the Site

Lamanai is open 8 A.M.–5 P.M. daily. Entrance costs US$10 per person. With the advent of midday cruise-ship tours, the site boasts a dock, a visitors center, craft shops, and a museum. Lamanai is also a popular site for day-trippers from Ambergris Caye, and it can be quite crowded in the middle of the day, especially during the week. For a more solitary experience, go early in the morning or late in the afternoon; cruise-ship crowds arrive at noon and disappear in less than two hours. To ensure a head start, stay at the award-winning **Lamanai Outpost Lodge** (tel. 501/220-9444, www.lamanai.com), a highly recommended one-of-a-kind jungle lodge.

In 2012

On June 16, 2012, the **Lamanai Challenge Triathlon** will involve canoeing, running, and cycling to other area sites, including La Milpa, Chan Chich, and Gallon Jug. Watch out for crocodiles.

Getting There

Lamanai is reachable by boat from **Orange Walk** or by road from **San Felipe.** Most visitors use one of the tour companies based in Orange Walk or the transfer services of a lodge, but it is possible to do it yourself as well. A two-person boat transfer from Orange Walk could cost as much as US$125, depending on the price of gasoline, less if you can get in with a bigger group. You can drive the San Felipe road in about 1.5 hours, depending on road conditions. Or take the village bus from Orange Walk to Indian Church, leaving Orange Walk at 5–6 P.M. on Fridays and Mondays. The same buses depart Indian Church at 5–5:30 A.M. on the same days, so you'll have to make a weekend out of it—or more. On the opposite end of the time, comfort, and price spectrum, you can charter a 15-minute flight from Belize City to Lamanai Outpost Lodge's airstrip with one of Belize's private charter services.

ALTUN HA

Altun Ha is the closest archaeological site to Belize City and the most accessible site in the country. Its main temple is famously depicted on the Belikin beer label. Altun Ha was a Maya trading center as well as a religious ceremonial site, which may have accommodated as many as 10,000 people. Archaeologists have dated

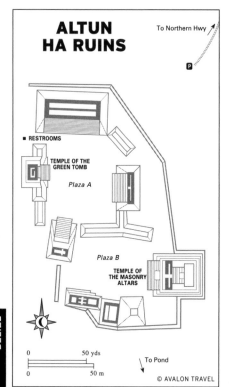

ALTUN HA RUINS

To Northern Hwy

P

RESTROOMS

TEMPLE OF THE
GREEN TOMB

Plaza A

Plaza B

TEMPLE OF
THE MASONRY
ALTARS

0   50 yds

0   50 m

To Pond

© AVALON TRAVEL

BELIZE

The concentration of structures includes palaces and temples surrounding two main plazas. The tallest building is the **Sun God Temple,** standing 59 feet above the plaza floor. At Altun Ha, the structure bases are oval and terraced. The small temples on top have small rooms built with the Maya trademark—the corbel arch.

Pendergast's team uncovered many valuable finds, including unusual green obsidian blades, pearls, and more than 300 jade pieces—beads, earrings, and rings. Seven funeral chambers were discovered, including the **Temple of the Green Tomb,** rich with human remains and traditional funerary treasures. Maya scholars believe the first man buried was someone of great importance. He was draped with jade beads, pearls, and shells. Next to his right hand lay the most exciting find: a solid jade head now referred to as **Kinich Ahau** ("The Sun God"), which is the largest jade carving found in any Maya country. The head weighs nine pounds and measures nearly six inches from base to crown. It is reportedly now housed in a museum in Canada.

Visiting the Site

Altun Ha is open 9 A.M.–5 P.M. daily. Entrance costs US$10. A gift shop and restrooms are at the entrance. Note that Altun Ha is a popular destination for cruise-ship passengers, so if you don't want to share your experience with 40 busloads of gawking cruisers, be sure to check with the park (tel. 501/609-3540) before arriving. In general, it's easy to avoid the crowds if you get there when the park first opens. You'll see more birds and wildlife that way as well.

A couple of local tour guides will be waiting at the entrance. They charge about US$10 per group per half hour and are well worth it. If you're coming to Altun Ha as part of a package, consider insisting that your tour provider use a local guide, to ensure that local communities receive something other than a crumbling road. To that end, also consider purchasing something from the independent artisans with crafts for sale.

construction to about 1,500–2,000 years ago. It wasn't until archaeologists came in 1964 that the old name "Rockstone Pond" was translated into the Maya words "Altun Ha." The site spans an area of about 25 square miles, most of which is covered by vegetation.

Altun Ha was rebuilt several times during the Preclassic, Classic, and Postclassic Periods. The desecration of the structures led scientists to believe that the site may have been abandoned because of violence.

A team led by Dr. David Pendergast of the Royal Ontario Museum began work in 1965 on the central part of the ancient city, where upwards of 250 structures have been found in an area of about 1,000 square yards. So far, this is the most extensively excavated of all the Maya sites in Belize.

Getting There

From **Belize City,** follow the Northern Highway north. Drive past the Burrell Boom turnoff (to the Baboon Sanctuary) and continue to about Mile 19, where the road forks; the right fork is the Old Northern Highway and leads to Altun Ha and **Maskall Village.** The entrance to Altun Ha is 10.5 miles from the intersection. The road is in horrible condition and is not getting any better with the increased traffic.

XUNANTUNICH

One of Belize's most impressive Maya ceremonial centers, and one of the crown jewels of the Cayo District, Xunantunich rests atop a natural limestone ridge with a grand view of the surrounding and Guatemalan countryside. The local name for the site, Xunantunich (shoo-NAHN-ta-nich), or "Stone Lady," is more common than the ancients' name for the site, Ka-at Witz, or "Supernatural Mountain," which was only recently discovered carved into a chunk of stone there.

Xunantunich is believed to have been built sometime around 400 B.C. and deserted around A.D. 1000; at its peak, some 7,000–10,000 Maya lived here.

Though certainly not the biggest of Maya structures, **El Castillo,** at 135 feet high, is the second-tallest pyramid in Belize. The eastern side of the structure displays an unusual stucco frieze (a reproduction); you can see three carved stelae in the plaza. Xunantunich contains three ceremonial plazas surrounded by house mounds.

Xunantunich was rediscovered in 1894, but not studied until 1938, by archaeologist Sir J. Eric Thompson. In 1950, the University of Pennsylvania (noted for its years of outstanding work across the border in Tikal) built a facility in Xunantunich for more study. In 1954, visitors were invited to explore the site after a road was opened and a small ferry built. In 1959, archaeologist Evan Mackie made news in the Maya world when he discovered evidence that part of Xunantunich had been destroyed by an earthquake in the Late Classic Period. Some

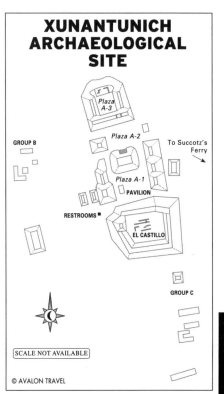

believe it was then that the people began to lose faith in their leaders. But for whatever reason, Xunantunich ceased to be a religious center long before the end of the Classic Period.

Visiting the Site

Xunantunich is open 8 A.M.–5 P.M. daily. Entrance costs US$10 per person. There are limited refreshments and souvenirs for sale. Guides (US$20 per group) are available and recommended, both to learn about what you're seeing and to support sustainable tourism. All guides are local and very knowledgeable.

In 2012

Xunantunich is the location of Belize's main event on December 21, 2012. There will be a festival, possibly with a concert and light show

BELIZE

on the ruins. This will be the finishing line for a youth torch run, in which torches will be brought to the site from the four directions, culminating in a fire ceremony to usher in the next 5,125 years.

Getting There

Xunantunich is located eight miles west of **San Ignacio.** The site is accessed by crossing the Río Mopan on the Succotz Ferry (8 A.M.–3 P.M. daily, free but tips appreciated), easily found on the Western Highway at the end of a line of crafts vendors. The hand-cranked ferry shuttles you (and your vehicle, if you have one) across the river. Afterwards you'll have about a mile's hike (or drive) up the hill to the site. Don't miss the 4 P.M. return ferry with the park rangers, or you'll be swimming.

EL PILAR

These jungle-choked Maya ruins are only visited by a handful of curious tourists each day; the rough approach road plus the lack of attention paid to the site by most tour operators helps make El Pilar the excellent, uncrowded day trip that it is. Two groupings of **temple mounds, courtyards,** and **ball courts** overlook a forested valley. Aqueducts and a causeway lead toward Guatemala, just 500 meters (1,640 feet) away. There have been some minor excavations here, including those by illegal looters, but the site is very overgrown, so the ruins retain an intriguing air of mystery.

Visiting the Site

El Pilar is remote, with no set hours. Entrance is US$10. Even if you book your El Pilar trip in San Ignacio, be sure to start your quest with a visit to the **Amigos del Pilar** visitors center (9 A.M.–5 P.M. daily) and **Be Pukte Cultural Center** in Bullet Tree Falls. Here you'll find a scale model of the ruins, some helpful booklets and maps, and guide and taxi arrangements.

The **Festival del Pilar** is planned for April 21, 2012.

Getting There

El Pilar is located seven miles north of **Bullet**

Tree Falls (nine miles from San Ignacio). It's about US$25 for a taxi from Bullet Tree Falls (the driver takes a group out and wait a few hours before taking them back). You can also rent a mountain bike or take a horseback ride at Cohune Palms and make a workout of it—the road's so bad, you'll probably beat the cab anyway.

ACTUN TUNICHIL MUKNAL

This is the acclaimed "Cave of the Crystal Maiden," one of the most spectacular natural and archaeological attractions in Central America. The trip to ATM, as the cave is also known, is for fit and active people who do not mind getting wet and muddy—and who are able to tread lightly around ancient artifacts. After the initial 45-minute hike to the entrance (with three river fords) and a swim into the cave's innards, you will be asked to remove your shoes upon climbing up the limestone into the main cathedral-like chambers. The rooms are littered with delicate Maya pottery and the crystallized remains of 14 humans. There are no pathways, fences, glass, or other partitions separating the visitor from the artifacts. Nor are there any installed lights. The only infrastructure is a rickety ladder leading up to the chamber of the Crystal Maiden herself, a full female skeleton that sparkles with calcite under your headlamp's glare, more so during the drier months.

Visting the Site

The site is found west of **Belmopan.** Entrance is US$25 per person. Only a few tour companies are licensed to take guests here; **Pacz Tours** (tel. 501/604-6921 or 501/824-0536, www.pacztours.net) is the most popular provider.

The Actun Tunichil Muknal cave is neither for the weak at heart nor recommended for small children or claustrophobics. In fact, children under the age of 8 (or 12, depending on whom you ask) are not permitted inside. Please be careful—the fact that tourists are allowed to walk here at all is as astonishing as the sights themselves (at the time of this writing,

© JOSHUA BERMAN

BELIZE

swimming into Actun Tunichil Muknal, the Cave of the Crystal Maiden

somebody had already trod on and broken one of the skulls).

CARACOL

Archaeologists Diane and Arlen Chase believe that Caracol, one of the largest sites in Belize, is the Maya city-state that toppled mighty Tikal, just to the northwest, effectively shutting it down for 130 years.

A former archaeological commissioner named the site "Caracol" ("snail" in Spanish) because of the winding logging road used to reach it, although some contend it was because of all the snail shells found during initial excavations. Caracol is *out there* and offers both natural wonders and Maya mystery. To date, only a small percentage of the 177 square kilometers (110 sq mi) that make up the site has even been mapped, identifying only 5,000 of the estimated 36,000 structures lying beneath the forest canopy.

The centerpiece is no doubt the pyramid of **Canaa,** which, at 136 feet above the plaza floor (roughly two meters higher than El Castillo

at Xunantunich), is one of the tallest structures—modern or ancient—in Belize. Canaa was only completely unveiled of vegetation in 2005, by the Tourism Development Project (TDP), whose work is responsible for most of the structures you see. The vistas from the top of Canaa are extensive and memorable.

In addition to the aforementioned superlatives, Caracol, a Classic Period site, is noted for its large masks and giant date glyphs on circular stone altars. There is also a fine display of the Maya's engineering skills, with extensive reservoirs, agricultural terraces, and several mysterious ramps.

Caracol has been studied for more than 20 years by the Chases and their assistants, student interns from Tulane University and the University of Central Florida. According to John Morris, an archaeologist with Belize's Institute of Archaeology, a lifetime of exploration remains to be done for six to nine miles in every direction of the excavated part of Caracol. It's proving to have been a powerful

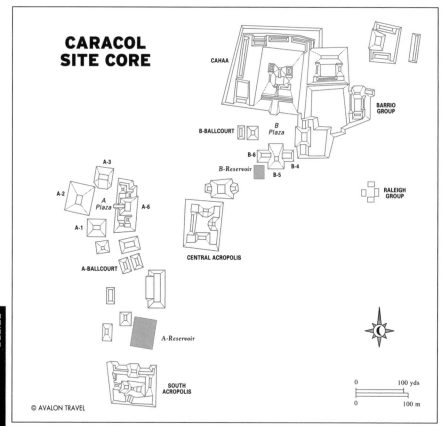

CARACOL SITE CORE

CAHAA

BARRIO GROUP

B-BALLCOURT

B Plaza

B-6

B-Reservoir

B-4

B-5

A-3

A-2

A Plaza

A-6

A-1

RALEIGH GROUP

A-BALLCOURT

CENTRAL ACROPOLIS

A-Reservoir

SOUTH ACROPOLIS

0   100 yds

0   100 m

© AVALON TRAVEL

BELIZE

site that controlled a very large area, with possibly over 100,000 inhabitants. The jungle you see now would have been totally absent in those days, the wood cleared to provide fuel and agricultural lands to support so many people.

Many carvings are dated A.D. 500–800, and ceramic evidence indicates that Caracol was settled around A.D. 300 and continued to flourish when other Maya sites were in decline. Carvings on the site also indicate that Caracol and Tikal engaged in ongoing conflicts, each defeating the other on various occasions. After the war in A.D. 562, Caracol flourished for more than a century in the mountains and valleys surrounding the site.

Visiting the Site

Caracol is open 8 A.M.–5 P.M. daily. Entrance is US$15. The visitors center has a scale model and interesting information based mostly on the work of the Chases over the last two decades. There are no official guides on-site, as most groups arrive with their own. However, the caretakers know Caracol well and will be glad to walk you through and explain the site for a few dollars. Most tours start with the Raleigh Group, move by the enormous ceiba trees, then circle through the archaeologists' camp and end with a bang by climbing Canaa. To prepare yourself—and to check on the latest discoveries and trail maps—go to www.caracol.org.

In 2012

Look for gatherings at Caracol to witness the vernal equinox (Mar. 20) and summer solstice (June 20) sunrise events in 2012. Cayo District lodges are sure to offer packages that include watching the sun come up over the E-Group in Plaza A.

Getting There

Caracol is located within the **Chiquibul Forest Reserve.** Most tour operators offer Caracol day trips, often involving stops at various caves and swimming holes on the way back through the Mountain Pine Ridge. A few, like **The Tut Brothers Caracol Shuttle** (tel. 501/610-5593 or 501/820-4014, caracolshuttle@hotmail.com), specialize in it; their shuttle leaves daily from Crystal Paradise Resort near Cristo Rey village and can pick up guests staying elsewhere in the area. The ride should take 2–3 hours, depending on both the weather and the progress made by road improvement crews, who hopefully will not run out of money before you read this. If you're driving, a 4WD vehicle is a must; gas is not available along the 50-mile road, so carry ample fuel. Camping is not allowed in the area without permission from the Institute of Archaeology in Belmopan. The closest accommodations are those along the Pine Ridge Road.

At times, a military escort is necessary to visit Caracol. Ask at your lodge. Tour operators know to show up at 9:30 A.M. at the Augustine (Douglas de Silva) gate to convoy to the ruins.

NIM LI PUNIT

Nim Li Punit is located in southern Belize, atop a hill with expansive views of the surrounding forests and mountains (it's about a half mile west of the highway, along a narrow road marked by a small sign). The site saw preliminary excavations in 1970 that documented a 30-foot-tall carved **stela,** the tallest ever found in Belize and among the tallest in all the Maya world. A total of about 25 stelae have been found on the site, most dated A.D. 700–800. Although looters damaged the site, excavations by archaeologist Richard Leventhal in 1986 and by the Belize Institute of Archaeology in the late 1990s and early 2000s uncovered several new stelae and some notable tombs.

Visiting the Site

Nim Li Punit is open 7 A.M.–5 P.M. daily. Entrance is US$5. The visitors center (tel. 501/665-5126) boasts an enormous stela and interesting artifacts.

Getting There

Nim Li Punit is located around Mile 75 on the Southern Highway, near the village of Indian Creek, 25 miles north of **Punta Gorda.** This is the closest archaeological site to Placencia, so day trips from there are available, and also from Punta Gorda Town.

LUBAANTUN

Lubaantun resides on a ridge between two creeks in southern Belize. Lubaantun ("Place of the Fallen Stones") consists of five layers of construction, unique from other sites because of the absence of engraved stelae. The site was first reported in 1875, by American Civil War refugees from the southern United States (who had fled here fearing vengeful Yankees), and first studied in 1915. It is believed that as many as 20,000 people lived in this trading center.

Lubaantun was built and occupied during the Late Classic Period (A.D. 730–890). Eleven major structures are grouped around five main plazas—in total the site has **18 plazas** and **three ball courts.** The tallest structure rises 50 feet above the plaza, and from it you can see the Caribbean Sea, 20 miles distant. Lubaantun's disparate architecture is completely different from Maya construction in other parts of Latin America.

Most of the structures are terraced, and you'll notice that some corners are rounded—an uncommon feature throughout the Mundo Maya. Lubaantun has been studied and surveyed several times by Thomas Gann and, more recently, in 1970, by Norman Hammond. Distinctive **clay whistle figurines** (similar to those found in Mexico's Isla Jaina) illustrate lifestyles and occupations of the era. Other artifacts include the mysterious **crystal skull,** obsidian blades,

BELIZE

BELIZE

THE SKULL OF DOOM

In 1924, Anna Mitchell-Hedges, the daughter of explorer F. A. Mitchell-Hedges, allegedly found a perfectly formed quartz crystal skull at the Lubaantun archaeological site on her 17th birthday. The object has been the subject of much mystery and controversy over the years. Was it made by the Maya a thousand years ago to conjure death? By aliens? By Atlanteans? Did Mitchell-Hedges plant it for the pleasure of his daughter? Is the whole story a hoax?

The world got its answer in 2007 when the Smithsonian Institute put the Mitchell-Hedges skull under a scanning electron microscope. Researcher Jane MacLaren Walsh concluded, "This object was carved and polished using modern, high-speed, diamond-coated, rotary, cutting and polishing tools of minute dimensions. This technology is certainly not pre-Columbian. I believe it is decidedly 20th century."

The skull currently resides in North America with the widower of Anna Mitchell-Hedges. Despite the Smithsonian's findings, some still warn of dire consequences if the skull is not returned to Lubaantun by December 21, 2012.

and shards of pottery. From all of this, archaeologists have determined that the city flourished until the 8th century A.D. It was a farming community that traded with the highland areas of today's Guatemala, and the people worked the sea and maybe the cayes just offshore.

Visiting the Site

Lubaantun is open 9 A.M.–5 P.M. daily. Entrance is US$10, payable at the visitors center located atop a hill a little more than a mile outside the village of San Pedro de Columbia. Ask the caretakers there about a guided tour, or just wander the ruins yourself and enjoy.

In 2012

In March 2012, Tumul K'in Maya Day will highlight the work of **Tumul K'in Learning Center** (www.tumulkinbelize.org), a nonprofit organization that promotes Maya values, knowledge, and philosophy. Also, look for a festival event here on December 21, 2012.

Getting There

Lubaantun is about 26 miles from **Punta Gorda.** Drive to the Southern Highway, then follow signs toward the village of San Pedro de Columbia and Lubaantun. Tour guides in Punta Gorda can also take you there. To reach the site by bus from Punta Gorda, take the San Miguel bus (departs 11 A.M. daily) and ask the driver to drop you at the entrance road to Lubaantun. It's a 20-minute uphill walk from there.

grinding stones (much like those still used today to grind corn), beads, shells, turquoise,

Tours and Packages

There are a huge range of packages offered by many of Belize's remarkable accommodations. As more hotels jump on the 2012 bandwagon, some may have nothing to do with the Maya or their calendar, except perhaps for their name or price tag. Others have prepared incredibly creative offerings to celebrate the year. When choosing your Maya package, be sure that at the very least, they are planning a special

tour of archaeological sites. Having Maya tour guides available for your day trips would also be good. A few properties are going over the top. The Lodge at Chaa Creek will re-create an ancient Maya village, where guests will participate by wearing Maya garb; and Black Orchid Resort, after five nights based on the river, will put guests in a rental car and send them off on their own Maya village expedition.

COMMUNITY TOURISM

Belize's Toledo District boasts several grass-roots tourism programs to get travelers into the upcountry villages of southern Belize. These villages are predominantly Q'eqchi' and Mopan Maya, whose descendants fled to Belize to escape oppression and forced labor in Guatemala. For the culturally curious traveler who doesn't mind relatively primitive conditions (which vary between villages), the unique experiential accommodation programs in the Toledo District are a great way to go. These are poor villages, and the local brand of eco-tourism provides an alternative to subsistence farming that entails slashing and burning the rainforest.

In addition to waking up to roosters crowing, you'll be guided to nearby natural attractions like caves, waterfalls, archaeological sites, and swimming holes. For nighttime entertainment, expect traditional dancing, singing, and music; otherwise it's just stargazing and conversation.

Homestays

Dem Dats Doin' (office in Punta Gorda located next to Scotia Bank, demdatsdoin@btl.net) has maintained the Maya Village Homestay Network since 1991, offering traditional village accommodations. Guests stay in a Maya home, perhaps in a hammock (not much privacy, but plenty of cultural exchange). The office in Punta Gorda is open only Wednesday and Friday mornings. It's less than US$20 per person per night for homestays and all meals. Families live in the villages of Aguacate, Na Luum Ca, and San José.

Maya Center

Maya Center is the gateway to the Cockscomb Basin Wildlife Sanctuary. Cockscomb Basin is one of the most beautiful natural attractions in the region. A large tract of approximately 155 square miles of forest was declared a forest reserve in 1984; in 1986, the government of Belize set the region aside as a preserve for the largest cat in the Americas, the jaguar. In the process, they relocated the Maya that were

living inside the reserve, forming the village of Maya Center. The area is alive with wildlife and there are a few families of guides and guesthouses to accommodate your needs.

The people of Maya Center struggle to support their town with tourism. The village has a few places to stay, eat, and experience village life, literally right down the road from the famous reserve.

Julio Saqui (www.cockscombmayatours.com) is a great guide and offers many services and tours including Victoria Peak. The Saqui family runs the **Maya Center Maya Museum** (tel. 501/660-3903 or 501/668-2194, US$10 pp), which provides hands-on cultural activities; learn how to make corn tortillas, process coffee beans, and take home Maya Coffee to share with friends while you retell your adventures abroad.

Nu'uk Che'il Cottages and Hmen Herbal Center (tel. 501/520-3033 or 501/615-2091, nuukcheil@btl.net, US$10–30) offers tranquil accommodations. The guesthouse has experience hosting student groups and can arrange seminars on herbal medicine, cultural performances, and the like. Proprietress Aurora Garcia Saqui offers Mayan spiritual blessings, prayer healings, acupuncture, and massage (each for less than US$15). Aurora can also arrange homestays in the village (US$30 includes a one-night stay with a local family, one dinner and one breakfast, per person).

Tutzil Nah Cottages (tel. 501/520-3044, www.mayacenter.com, US$14–22) is owned and operated by the Chun family. Inventive trips are available, including kayak floats and night hikes.

Red Bank

In Belize, "bed-and-breakfast" sometimes means a simple village homestay—crashing in a family's guest room. Tucked away on a red dirt road, the Mopan Maya village of Red Bank is famous for an annual local aggregation of scarlet macaws, which gather to feed on the ripe fruits of polewood trees. This phenomenon was unknown to outsiders until 1997, when conservationists learned that 20 birds had been hunted for table fare. (At that time it

CALENDAR OF EVENTS

Following is a preliminary look at the evolving and growing calendar of events for Belize in 2012. For more information, visit www.travel belize.org.

JANUARY

- January 11: The **Scientific Achievements of the Mayas** lecture presentation for the official launch at the Bliss Center for the Performing Arts in Belize City. Led by Dr. Jaime Awe, director of the Institute of Archaeology, this lecture will focus on scientific achievements of the Maya.

- January 21: **Maya Palace Feast at Cahal Pech** in San Ignacio. There will be performances by local indigenous groups including Euphoria Dance Group, Pablo Collado, and marimba music, all at the archaeological site of Cahal Pech 1-5 P.M. This used to be a royal palace, so the feast is on – expect local and indigenous food.

- January 25: **Traditional Healers Conference and Workshop** at the George Price Conference Room in Belmopan. The conference will bring together Maya healers from all over the country to discuss traditional practice and to chart a way forward.

FEBRUARY

- February 14: **Maya Love Classic Across the Heartland.** This a popular annual cycling race across the width of Belize.

- February 18: **Altun Ha Maya Fest and Kinich Ahau Art Exhibition.** The village of Rockstone Pond hosts a fun festival at the site of Altun Ha, with local crafts, food and drink, entertainment, and exhibits.

MARCH

- March 8-11: **La Ruta Maya River Challenge** (www.larutamayabelize.com). This is Belize's Super Bowl, an exciting and convivial canoe race held during the first week of March and timed to coincide with Baron Bliss Day celebrations. San Ignacio is the start of the race, where you'll see 100 teams of paddlers amass in the Macal River then bolt downstream – racing five days down the 173-mile length of the Belize River, all the way to Belize City. They do it in timed sections, camping at designated spots along the way. It is, in fact, the same route that the Maya used for their trade and commerce since 2,000 years ago.

- March 20: **Equinox at Caracol.** Catch the sun rising over the E-Group in Plaza A.

APRIL

- April: **San José Succotz Fiesta.** An annual fair held at the western village of San José Succotz in honor of their patron Saint

was thought Belize had a population of 30–60 scarlet macaws!) In response, Programme for Belize worked with the village council to form the Red Bank Scarlet Macaw Conservation Group, led by village leader Geronimo Sho.

The small community-based eco-tourism industry offers visitors accommodation, meals, crafts, and guide services. A reserve has been established about one mile from the village and visitors must pay a small conservation fee (ask around for Mr. Sho). The best time to visit is from mid-January to March, when the annatto fruits are ripe. As many as 100 scarlet macaws have been observed in the morning when the birds are feeding. To stay here, make a reservation at the **Red Bank Bed-and-Breakfast** (tel. 501/503-2233).

Toledo Ecotourism Association (TEA)

TEA is a cooperatively managed tourism program with village representatives and guesthouses in seven participating villages. Participants must arrange their visits from

Joseph. There will be a hog head dance, traditional food, music, and dance.

- April 21: **Fiesta del Pilar** in Bullet Tree Falls.

MAY

- May: **National Agriculture and Trade Show.** Held in Belmopan, the show features Maya cultural performances and a Maya 2012 booth showcasing agricultural and other Maya products.

- May 18: **Toledo Cacao Fest.** An annual ode and party celebrating all things chocolate. It lasts all weekend long and is worth going to in any year.

JUNE

- June 4-6: **Belize Archaeological Symposium** at the National Institute of Culture and History. Held for all professional archaeological researchers to share their findings. Papers are compiled and published in an annual volume; anyone is invited to sit in on the lectures and presentations.

- June 16: **Lamanai Challenge Triathlon.** Canoeing, running, and cycling between archaeological sites in northern Belize. Run from La Milpa to Chan Chich, cycle to Gallon Jug, paddle the New River to Lamanai. This is possibly the only triathlon in the world where you can encounter jaguars and crocodiles!

- June 20: **Solstice at Caracol.**

SEPTEMBER

- September 22: **Autumnal equinox at Caracol.**

OCTOBER

- October 19-21: **World Indigenous Music Festival.** Brings together indigenous groups from around the world to perform in an "indigenous musical cultural explosion."

NOVEMBER

- November 26: **History, Socio-Anthropological and Cultural Symposium.** Held for researchers and professionals in these disciplines to present papers and findings.

DECEMBER

- December 21: **Closing event at Cahal Pech.** Expect performances, indigenous music, cultural dances, marimba music, a fire ceremony, food, and drinks.

- December 21-23: **Lubaantun Musical Festival Baktun 13.**

- December 22-23: **Fire Ceremony and Gala Event at Xunantunich.** An overnight event to bring in the 21st, featuring a Youth Torch Run from North, South, and Eastern Maya temples to an epicenter and then into Xunantunich.

BELIZE

the central TEA office in Punta Gorda (tel. 501/722-2096, www.plenty.org/mayan-ecotours), pay the registration fee (US$5), then be briefed about the program and told how to get out to the village (villages participate on a rotating basis). One full day may be sufficient, as the villages are quite small; to explore the surrounding landscape, plan an extra day.

One night's lodging and three meals run US$28 per person per night. Other activities, like storytelling, crafts lessons, and village tours, are US$3.50 per hour. Prices are standardized throughout the participating villages. Other activities, such as paddling trips, forest and cave tours, and music/dance sessions cost more, but are extremely reasonable—especially with a group. If visiting during the rainy season, be advised that trails and caves may be inaccessible.

Breakfast in Maya villages generally consists of eggs, homemade tortillas, and coffee or a cacao drink. Lunch is the largest meal of the day, often including chicken *caldo,* a soup cooked with Maya herbs, or occasionally a local meat dish like iguana ("bush chicken") or gibnut (paca, a large rodent).

TOURS IN 2012

The Mayan Traveler (tel. 888/843-6292 or 713/299-5665, www.themayantraveler. com) is a tour company with trips throughout the Mundo Maya, including a six-night **Archaeology Tour plus Tikal** featuring lectures on the Maya calendar and the possibility of a new cycle. Guests visit Lamanai, Xunantunich, Caracol, Cahal Pech, and Tikal, where they will spend the night. The morning is free to wander the city in the jungle.

Chocolate Tours

Cotton Tree Lodge (tel. 501/621-8776) offers special weeklong chocolate packages and produces its own small-batch chocolate bars and cacao juice. They are very creative and partner with **Sustainable Harvest International** (tel. 501/722-2010, U.S. tel. 207/669-8254, www.sustainableharvest.org),

a nonprofit organization working to alleviate poverty and deforestation throughout Central America. In 2012, Cotton Tree Lodge will offer a chocolate package around Valentine's Day in February, then again for the Cacao Fest in May.

There are many chocolate tours based out of Punta Gorda all year long, but hard-core chocolate lovers will want to plan their trip around **Cacao Fest** (www.toledochocolate. com), held over the Commonwealth Day holiday weekend in late May, and celebrating all things chocolate—from chocolate kisses to cacao martinis.

HOTEL PACKAGES
Belize District

Maruba Resort (tel. 501/225-5555, U.S. tel. 800/627-8227, www.maruba-belize.com, US$130–700 per night) has a **Maya Afterlife Adventure Tour** (US$1,199 per person) with trips to Altun Ha, Lamanai, Actun Tunichil Muknal, and with exclusive access to Mammy

Learn the entire process of chocolate making.

© JOSHUA BERMAN

BELIZE

Ridge archaeological site, where you can crawl into an unexcavated royal Maya tomb.

Black Orchid Resort (2 Dawson Ln., Burrell Boom Village, tel. 501/225-9158, www.blackorchidresort.com, US$975–1,125 per person based on double occupancy) is going with the apocalyptic theme to describe their **Belize It 2012** package. ("We can think of nowhere better to end it all than where the elders predicted it thousands of years ago.") An interesting seven-night package includes five nights in a spacious room at the fully equipped riverside resort, plus two nights in the Toledo District, where you'll follow a self-directed tour and stay in a Maya village. The week includes one Maya dinner at Black Orchid Restaurant, a trip to Actun Tunichil Muknal, and—my favorite—a full-day private tour of Lamanai archaeological zone, one of the most stunning sites in all of the Mundo Maya.

Ambergris Caye

At **Portofino Beach Resort** (tel. 501/226-5096, www.portofinobelize.com, US$250–350), an Ambergris Caye property, their seven-night **2012 Doomsday Package** (Dec. 15–22, US$2,305 per person double occupancy) offers "front-row seats" to the end of the world—or the dawn of the new era. The package includes all breakfasts and dinners, including one night of Mayan buffet, a trip to Xunantunich, cave tubing, snorkeling, and a trip to Lamanai.

Vicinity of San Ignacio

One of the region's premiere jungle lodges, **The Lodge at Chaa Creek** (tel. 877/709-8708, www.chaacreek.com, US$3,563 per adult) is located in between the country's two largest and most important archaeological sites: Xunantunich and Caracol. Chaa Creek is offering a **Belize Maya Heartland 2012 Adventure Vacation** and, for the solstice itself, a seven-night all-inclusive **Maya Winter Solstice 2012** (Dec. 15–22). Chaa Creek's celebrations will focus on "factual information,

Pook's Hill, one of many jungle lodges in Belize offering a special 2012 package, is built amid an unexcavated Maya plaza and is surrounded by protected forests.

cultural integrity, and respect for the people of this vibrant civilization."

They are putting on a festive week that is also educational. Guests will learn about ancient and contemporary Maya culture through daily on-site lectures on Maya cosmology, spiritualism, astrology, astronomy, and a range of other themes. Chaa Creek guests participating in the 2012 winter solstice program will receive loose, white traditional Maya attire, as well as a carved talisman with their birth-date glyph. A huge stela will be erected on December 22 "with the names or glyphs of participating guests inscribed on it."

The highly rated, horseback-centric jungle lodge **Mountain Equestrian Trails** (tel. 800/838-3918 or 501/669-1124, metbelize@pobox.com, www.metbelize.com) has a **2012 Maya Land Adventure** ($1,850 per person, double occupancy). The trip begins with a full-day horseback ride to the Barton Creek Cave, a sacred place used by the Maya for agricultural and fertility rites, ritual bloodletting, human sacrifice, and lineage internment. The rest of the week includes immersion in nature, ceramic making, and a trip to Tikal and the nearby butterfly farm. They are also offering a Skeptics Package for December 21, 2012.

Pook's Hill (tel. 501/820-2017, www.pookshillbelize.com, US$198) is a unique, isolated jungle resort built into the hillside amid an actual Maya archaeological site. They have a seven-day **Year of the Maya** tour package whose themes include herbal medicine from the jungle, Q'eqchi' and Mopan Maya cooking, archaeology, discussions about the Maya calendar, storytelling, and copal-burning ceremonies. Guests spend six nights at Pook's

Hill, with tours to Xunantunich, Caracol, and Cahal Pech archaeological sites, morning forest walks, a trip to nearby Actun Tunichil Muknal cave, and a day trip to Tikal. Package prices from January to May and for December are US$3,150 for two people; the rate is reduced to US$2,680 during low season (June–Nov.). There are a number of ways to customize your trip, including an overnight at Tikal.

Ka'ana Boutique Hotel & Spa (tel. 501/824-3350, www.kaanabelize.com, US$250–350) is kicking things up a few notches with **The Maya: A Journey Through Time,** featuring a full-on rock-star tour of the Caracol archaeological site. Get this: Guests fly in to the site by helicopter, skimming over the forests and Mountain Pine Ridge, then get a personal tour of the site while your personal chef prepares dinner amid the ruins. A luxury overnight camp is made atop the 140-foot-high Caana temple. After a night under the stars, enjoy breakfast in the ruins before your helicopter flight back to the resort. I guess you only live once. The package (US$22,000 per person) also includes energy work with a Maya shaman and an exclusive cave trip with the director of archaeology.

Placencia

Across the country, **Chabil Mar** (tel. 866/417-2377, www.chabilmar.com) is a high-end beach resort in Placencia offering a seven-night **Maya of Belize Immersion.** Their immersion includes an introductory seminar on Maya history and visits to archaeological sites, as well as to two Maya villages "to learn Maya farming techniques, crafts, food, cooking, and medicine." The licensed tour guide is from the Mopan Maya Village of Red Bank.

HONDURAS

I first arrived in Copán on a Friday afternoon, traveling with a group of university students on a service-learning summer program. We pulled into the town of Copán Ruinas in a drizzle. We were excited to tour the famous site in the morning, but first we gathered on the flat roof of our guesthouse to watch the sunset across the Valle de Copán. For an hour, the sky eased through pastels and we took it in, trying to imagine 20,000 Maya walking in this valley 1,000 years ago.

As we softly talked, the sky darkened and someone pointed out Venus, one of the most important sky deities, especially in Copán. We would see Venus depicted on carved masks in the morning and would learn how the Maya timed their wars with Venus's cycles. But for now, we could only look at the planet from our perch on that rooftop. Before even setting foot in the ruins we felt their importance, in the sky and in the warm evening air.

The next morning we wandered the ruins, stunned not only by the carvings, tunnels, and layered dynasties, but also by the tranquility. Neatly trimmed lawns connected clusters of ancient attractions, which we climbed and inspected.

Honduras's slice of the Mundo Maya is miniscule compared to the other countries, but what it lacks in quantity, it makes up for with one word: Copán.

HISTORY

Copán's history is concisely documented on Altar Q, the famous lineage monument in front of the Acropolis with 16 kings in a row,

© AMY E. ROBERTSON

each handing power to the other down the line. The area had been inhabited for centuries, but never consolidated under a strong, single dynasty the way it was when K'inich Yax K'uk' Mo', or Great-Sun First Quetzal Macaw, arrived from the nation of Tikal. His ascension to the throne coincided with the ending of the 8th *b'aktun* and beginning of the 9th, giving Yax K'uk' Mo' supernatural powers in the eyes of the people. That his dynasty lasted 16 generations—400 years, another complete *b'aktun*—further strengthened the importance of long-cycle endings to the Maya. An excellent PBS/NOVA special called *Lost King of the Maya* tells the story of the discovery of Yax K'uk' Mo's 1,600-year-old, 130-foot-deep grave.

Copán collapsed with the end of the Classic Period in A.D. 900, consumed by the jungle, known only to locals and wildlife until gringo explorers John Lloyd Stephens and Frederick Catherwood recorded some of the longest lasting descriptions and images (Catherwood made fantastically detailed line drawings) ever produced of the place.

Stephens wrote of their approach, their guide slashing with his machete until they reached "fourteen monuments of the same character and appearance, some with more elegant designs, and some in workmanship equal to the finest monuments of the Egyptians; one displaced from its pedestal by enormous roots; another locked in the close embrace of branches of trees, and almost lifted out of the earth; another hurled to the ground, and bound down by huge vines and creepers; and one standing, with its altar before it, in a grove of trees which grew around it, seemingly to shade and shroud it as a sacred thing; in the solemn stillness of the woods, it seemed a divinity mourning over a fallen people. The only sounds that disturbed the quiet of this buried city were the noise of monkeys moving among the tops of the trees."

In Copán, this mood still stands. The city's last Long Count date was A.D. 822. The rest is history.

PLANNING YOUR TIME

Copán is located in the northwestern corner of Honduras, a three-hour drive from the international airport at San Pedro Sula, or a six-hour ride from Guatemala City. Copán is a premiere attraction for all of Honduras, yet compared to other major archaeological sites in the Mundo Maya, it receives only a fraction of the tourists.

Spend at least three days in the ruins and surrounding area, making sure to visit at different times of the day to see the same structures in a different light.

You can extend a trip to Copán for weeks, since the territory surrounding the archaeological site features rainforests, Chortí Maya and Lencan villages, and the colonial town of Santa Rosa de Copán. **Copán Ruinas** town is more convenient for early-morning ruin tours (the best time to visit any ruin) and is far more charming, with coffee, guesthouses, and Saint Day festivals.

There is plenty to do in the area besides visit the ruins. This is the gateway to some of Honduras's most mountainous adventures. Head to the pueblo of Gracias to embark on some truly unique trekking and community tourism opportunities, or find a jungle spa or sweat lodge and just relax as the calendar clicks on.

In 2012

An official **Comité de Copán 2012** formed in 2011 to coordinate local businesses and interests planning for the important calendar event of 2012. There will be various fairs celebrating Lenca Maya culture, events programmed around each solstice and equinox date, deer dances, plays, and a big fair surrounding the winter solstice.

The **Maya Festival Copán** (Dec. 18–23, info@seedoflightcopan.com) is a full-on feast of Maya culture and festivities. Book your room *now* to get a front-row seat for archaeological seminars, fire ceremonies, mass meditation, musical presentations, and children's activities. (Copán is not a big place; I've heard reports of rooms filling up more than a year in advance.)

Maya Archaeological Sites

The city of Copán was far and away the artistic leader of all the Maya cities, with ornate sculptures and statues, and the most complete hieroglyphic historical record yet found. The ruins of Copán and smaller surrounding sites, located in a lovely river valley, are worth at least two days, more for the archaeology buff. Don't miss a trip to the sculpture museum, with a full-scale painted replica of an ancient temple in the center, or Las Sepulturas, for a glimpse of Maya daily life.

COPÁN

Once called "the Athens of the New World" for its 400-year reign as the Maya world's undisputed cultural, artistic, and architectural center, Copán is also notable for its depth. Each new king would carefully bury the previous ruler's monuments and then build his own on top of them. A thousand years later, archaeologists

have tunneled down into this dynasty, a labyrinth that continues to produce discoveries.

Copán was *classic* Classic Period: empires, deadly ball games, kingly propaganda, and the empire's most skilled artists and scribes. Copán doesn't have the sheer height and grandeur of Tikal, its rival to the west, but it makes up for it in details and mystique.

Copán contains a reference to 3114 B.C., the beginning of the Long Count cycle that ends in 2012. It is also on the same latitude as Izapa, the birthplace of the Long Count, and its artwork depicts astronomy-guided images similar to the galactic alignment.

The Ruins

Copán's highlights include an early-morning walking tour of the Great Plaza, with its open lawn and freestanding stelae depicting the city's history.

© AMY E. ROBERTSON

HONDURAS

The renowned "Altar Q" depicts the 16 rulers of the Copán dynasty.

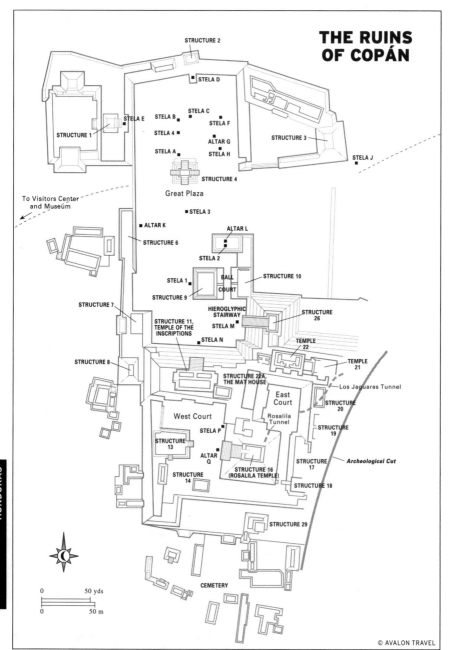

THE RUINS OF COPÁN

STRUCTURE 2

STELA D

STRUCTURE 1
STELA E
STELA B
STELA C
STELA 4
STELA F
ALTAR G
STELA A
STELA H
STRUCTURE 4

STRUCTURE 3
STELA J

To Visitors Center and Museúm

Great Plaza

STELA 3
ALTAR K
STRUCTURE 6
ALTAR L
STELA 2
STELA 1
BALL COURT
STRUCTURE 10
STRUCTURE 9

STRUCTURE 7
STRUCTURE 11, TEMPLE OF THE INSCRIPTIONS
HIEROGLYPHIC STAIRWAY
STELA M
STRUCTURE 26
STELA N
TEMPLE 22
STRUCTURE 8
TEMPLE 21
STRUCTURE 22A, THE MAT HOUSE
Los Jaguares Tunnel
East Court
STRUCTURE 20
West Court
STELA P
Rosalila Tunnel
STRUCTURE 19
STRUCTURE 13
ALTAR Q
STRUCTURE 17
Archeological Cut
STRUCTURE 14
STRUCTURE 16 (ROSALILA TEMPLE)
STRUCTURE 18

STRUCTURE 29

CEMETERY

0   50 yds
0   50 m

© AVALON TRAVEL

On **Stela C,** a ruler from the 8th century, 18 Rabbit, is depicted as a sun god standing in a caiman's jaw, a symbol of the dark rift in the Milky Way. Author and researcher John Major Jenkins says this is a reference to the 2012 alignment of the solstice sun and the center of the Milky Way. (Similar to Izapa, where glyphs of the sun, Venus, the ecliptic, the Milky Way, and the dark rift also point toward 2012.)

The **Hieroglyphic Stairway** lies on the western face of the pyramid and was built in A.D. 753 by Smoke Shell. This one-of-a-kind structure contains more than 2,500 glyphs, emblems, and name glyphs from Copán's history from A.D. 700. A tomb lies beneath these stairs, as well as several ceremonial rooms.

The **Acropolis** is another vast network of structures where astounding discoveries have been made. **Altar Q** lies in the West Court and depicts 16 seated kings carved around all four sides of a stone monument. Under the East Court lies the **tomb of Yax K'uk' Mo'** and his wife. **Structure 16** was the site of Copán's biggest discovery: Moon Jaguar's **Rosalila Temple,** found in 1989. The Rosalila Temple actually lies beneath Structure 16; a full replica is in the on-site museum. Upon discovery, it was considered one of the best-preserved ceremonial spaces ever found in the Maya world.

About a mile through the trees from the Acropolis, **Las Sepulturas** served as a residential area for Copán. Because of the grand limestone causeway connecting this area to the temple site, this may have served as a kind of suburban neighborhood of elite Maya.

Visiting the Site

Copán and its museum are open 8 A.M.–4 P.M. daily. Entrance to the main park plus Las Sepulturas is US$15; the **Museo de Escultura Maya** (Maya Sculpture Museum) is another US$7. Both are highly recommended. Most of Copán's best monuments and artifacts are actually in the Museo de Escultura Maya, so save time for a visit here. It costs another US$15 to enter the tunnels (a little pricey, but you should get the full experience while you're here). Amy E. Robertson, author of *Moon Honduras,* offers the following advice:

- It can be very nice to get in right when the gates open. In the early-morning hours, you'll be able to enjoy the ruins in relative solitude, and you'll have good low-angle light for photographs. This is also the favorite time for a group of white-tailed deer that live in the woods to come out and wander through the ruins.

- When walking around the site, refrain from walking on stairways that have been roped off.

- Try not to lean on sculptures, stelae, or buildings—salts from your skin can corrode the stone, especially when multiplied by the 60,000 or so visitors who come to Copán each year.

- It should go without saying, but let it be said: It is illegal to remove any stones from the park.

- Two pamphlet-guides to the ruins are sold at the ticket office: *History Carved in Stone,* by William Fash and Ricardo Agurcia Fasquelle, and *Copán, Legendario y Monumental,* by J. Adan Cueva. The former, written in English, has an excellent interpretation of the growth of the city and advances in archaeology, but does not discuss each monument individually. The latter, in English and Spanish, is weak on recent advances in archaeology, and although it does give descriptions of many major sites, they are often incomplete and not entirely useful.

- Guides can be hired at the site for US$25 for a two-hour tour. Some of these local men have worked at the ruins for many years and have a positively encyclopedic knowledge about the archaeology of Copán—not just the names of buildings, but explanations on how archaeological views changed, when certain discoveries were made and why they were important, and all sorts of other details. In addition to providing information on the ruins themselves, guides often relate interesting local legends and

HONDURAS

Q&A: DR. EDWIN BARNHART, ARCHAEOLOGIST

Archaeologist, explorer, and instructor Ed Barnhart, PhD, has been traveling in the Mesoamerican jungles for decades. His involvement in Maya studies began in 1990 as an archaeological intern in Copán, Honduras, and continued in Belize, where he discovered the Maya ruins of Ma'ax Na. In 1996 he was invited back to Copán, where he found himself witnessing – and participating in – one of the biggest discoveries of the century. Dr. Barnhart's Palenque mapping project added some 1,100 new structures to the site map, which has been celebrated as "one of the most detailed and accurate ever made of a Maya ruin." Today, Dr. Barnhart serves as the director of the Maya Exploration Center (MEC, www.mayaexploration. org), a nonprofit organization dedicated to the study of ancient Maya civilization.

When did you first travel to a Mundo Maya country, and how did it impact you?
I first went to Copán, Honduras, in 1990 as a field school student of Bill Fash, now the Boditch Chair of Harvard but then a professor at Northern Illinois University. My father said I was an idiot for signing up for the field school, pointing out that I had never even been out of the country. Honduras?
    I worked as a dishwasher at the dorms at CU

Boulder to make the money and landed in Honduras in June of 1990. The month was great, and I was there when the excavations found nine eccentric flints in the Rosalila building in the tunnels. National Geographic showed up, and I was swept up in the importance of the find. Linda Schele was there, and she so impressed me that I went to UT Austin to become one of her students studying Mayan hieroglyphics.

What advice do you have for someone traveling to a Maya village or archaeological site for the first time?
I would say be respectful, [be] yourself, and treat [the Maya] as equals. Most Maya speak Spanish now, and many at the sites want to learn English. Maya society is very open and they love making friends. In Mexico, they are often treated as second-class citizens because they are "indios," and a little bit of interest in their culture and honest friendliness is returned with kindness.

Do you know of any specific places or programs, especially community-based tourism efforts, that empower Maya villagers?
Cobá and Palenque both have strong associations of Maya tour guides, who speak about

tall tales about the area. Casual tourists may find their brains spinning with the endless stories of temples, rulers, and altars, but if you're really curious to learn more about Copán, you are definitely encouraged to hire a guide. They charge an extra US$10 to accompany you to the Sculpture Museum, and US$15 for Las Sepulturas—both worthwhile expenses.

• Although English-speaking guides are available, their language abilities vary. If your Spanish is nonexistent, check beforehand to make sure you and your guide can communicate well. You may want to consider contacting the **Asociación de Guías Copán**

(tel. 504/651-4018, guiascopan@yahoo. com) ahead of your visit to reserve a guide in English, particularly during high season (Holy Week, July and August). Guides are available in a number of other languages as well.

Getting There
San Pedro Sula is three hours away and has an airport. You can also take a six-hour bus ride from Guatemala City to Copán. Several express bus services make regular runs from San Pedro Sula to Copán Ruinas. Hedman Alas has four daily buses, and Casasola Express has three daily buses.

COURTESY OF EDWIN BARNHART

Dr. Ed Barnhart (pictured here at Yaxhá, in Guatemala) began his career in archaeology with a trip to Copán.

their ancestors in a very real way. Visiting the Lacandón in Chiapas and having them guide you out to the remote ruins of Lacanja is also a very real experience. Bonampak is run by the Lacandón as well. In the highlands of Guatemala, you can often see modern Maya performing ceremonies in ruins like Iximche, Utatlán, and Zacuelo.

What has been your most memorable moment so far traveling in the Mundo Maya?
Dawn on top of Temple IV at Tikal; the remote ruins along the Pasión river; and witnessing a Maya ceremony at Quiriguá. Actually, perhaps seeing hundreds of Maya flood into the plaza of Tikal to honor the dead of Lake Atitlán's horrible mudslides in October of 2008 was the most memorable experience. [Watching] shamans lead their communities around and telling the stories of the stelae there was very touching.

Do you have any travel plans in the year 2012?
I'll be in Palenque. My extended family has asked me to arrange a family trip for Christmas to Palenque, and I will probably do that. I personally think we have misunderstood the Maya calendar, and 2012 is a benchmark rather than an end.

Tours and Packages

COMMUNITY TOURISM

The **Copán Maya Foundation** (tel. 504/2651-4103, www.copanmaya.org) is a far-reaching nonprofit organization that works in tandem with Copán Association (www.asociacioncopan.org), a Honduran nonprofit organization. Together they support research, archaeology, natural-resource management, and education in the area. They helped establish the Copán Sculpture Museum, reforestation of the site, clean-water initiatives, and macaw-preservation efforts. They also facilitated the creation of the Casa K'inich Children's Museum in Copán. Online educational offerings include a bilingual teachers manual for the Casa K'inich Children's Museum, lessons on the preservation of the scarlet macaw, and a bilingual "Manual de Monumentos de Copán." Casa K'inich is always in need of patrons to help out with the upkeep of their projects.

TOURS IN 2012

Copán Connections (www.copanconnections. com) creates custom trips throughout Honduras. Or choose from a variety of tours, which will take you to the Copán ruins and beyond.

EL SALVADOR

El Salvador has many Maya archaeological sites, but few are as big or accessible as the sites in other countries. The **Fundación Nacional de Arqueología de El Salvador** (FUNDAR, National Foundation of Archaeology of El Salvador, www.fundar.sv.org) is the only nongovernmental organization in the country dedicated to the conservation, protection, and investigation of Salvadoran archaeology. FUNDAR has worked with the Salvadoran cultural ministry to help establish the administration, protection, and development of the country's archaeological parks, which include Cihuatán, Joya de Cerén, San Andrés, Tazumal, and Casa Blanca. Salvador's Maya sites are absent of important inscriptions. Most sites are in the western part of the country; in the east, the only accessible site is the Gruta de Espiritu Santo, with ancient petroglyphs. San Salvador has many direct flights since it is the hub for TACA Airlines, and it is fairly easy to get around the country.

HOTEL PACKAGES

The *temazcal,* or Maya sweat lodge, is a purification ritual that uses the earth's four elements: earth, air, water, and fire. Experience a *temazcal* in the middle of a Honduran coffee forest at **Spa Ixchel** (8 km south, Hacienda San Isidro, Copán Ruinas, tel. 504/9708-1584, www.spaixchel.com), 25 minutes from the Copán ruins. Named for the Maya fertility and moon goddess, Spa Ixchel offers a full range of therapies and spa services, plus healthy Honduran food. The spa offers a discount of 15 percent for 2012.

Seed of Light Holistic Services (tel. 504/9888-5057, www.seedoflightcopan.com) will host several special 2012 yoga retreats, wellness packages, and "healing vibrations," all set in Copán Ruinas. Retreats serve individuals, small groups, group leaders, and "spiritual adventure seekers."

Hacienda San Lucas (tel. 504/2651-4495, info@haciendasanlucas.com, www.haciendasanlucas.com) is an eco-lodge in a 100-year-old ranch overlooking the ruins, which *Yoga Journal* says offered "a fusion of Mayan philosophy and Kripalu yoga." The hotel will host yoga and meditation retreats—stoking up the *temazcal,* playing music, and visiting hot springs.

HONDURAS

BACKGROUND

History

THE EARLIEST RESIDENTS

The oldest human yet discovered in the Western Hemisphere was found in 2008 in an underwater cave complex in the Yucatán, about 27 miles southwest of Tulum. Named the "Eve of Naharón" by her discoverers, she dates to the year 11,600 B.C., or 10,000 years before the peninsula became the heart of the Maya world. In those days, Ice Age humans hunted woolly mammoth and other large animals roaming the cool, moist landscape of Mexico and Central America (you can visit their bones in Loltun Cave). Eventually, these Archaic peoples, as they are known, settled into villages, some of which became precursors to Maya cities.

PRECLASSIC

After about 1000 B.C., the Olmec, Zapotec, and early Maya cultures formed in various parts of Mesoamerica. These cultures developed the New World's first calendar system and an early system of writing, the knowledge of which spread throughout Mesoamerica. "As the Olmec influence moved from Veracruz south to Chiapas," writes Michael Coe in his classic text *The Maya*, "use of hieroglyphic writing and calendar keeping followed." It first appeared in Izapa and Tak'alik Ab'aj, along the Pacific Coast, before venturing into the Guatemala highlands, then reaching the Preclassic cities of the Petén—Tikal, Yaxhá, and El Mirador.

© JOSHUA BERMAN

WHY THE MAYA SETTLED IN MESOAMERICA

There are several reasons why Archaic roamers decided to stop hunting and gathering and to start farming and staying put in Mesoamerica – reasons that explain not only why they survived here, but why they thrived and developed such a great culture as the Maya.

The switch from hunter to farmer occurred gradually between 7000 B.C. and 2000 B.C. The people learned to raise corn, beans, squash, and chili peppers, the mainstay of the Mesoamerican diet even today. In fact, the people of the Mundo Maya – in the Balsas River basin, to be exact – are believed to be the first in the world to develop and use maize, or corn, which they bred from a weak, weedy predecessor called *teosinte*.

Another reason they could stay was limestone. The same material that they would eventually cut into blocks and make into plaster for their temples first served as a dietary additive. Ancient Mesoamericans ground powdered white lime with dried corn, a process called *nixtamal*, which allowed them to balance the amino acids in their corn and add niacin, essential to a human's diet.

Finally, there was salt. By harvesting exportable salt from lagoons on the Yucatán's north coast, the people there controlled a valuable substance that was in fact crucial for Maya cities to flourish and grow in the jungles to the south. As elite classes created new demands, they traded salt for precious commodities from the south, like jade, exotic bird feathers, shells, obsidian, and cacao (Michael Coe writes that a city the size of Tikal, which housed about 45,000 people, would have had to import 131 tons of salt each year).

These kingdoms pushed northward into the Yucatán, where the use of the Long Count arrived around A.D. 250, the beginning of the golden age of Maya civilization.

THE CLASSIC PERIOD

The Classic Period is defined as the period during which the Long Count was used in the lowland Yucatán area—A.D. 250–900. The Maya made phenomenal progress in the development of artistic, architectural, and astronomical skills during these 650 glory years—for the ruling classes, anyway. (Someone else had to work the limestone and build those pyramids.) The Maya of this era constructed kingdoms and wrote codices (folded bark books) filled with hieroglyphic symbols that detailed complicated calculations of days, months, years, and greater cycles of time.

These are the years that gave the Maya their reputation as thinkers, philosophers, and astronomers. In *Time Among the Maya*, author Ronald Wright describes these Maya as "the Greeks of the New World, living in warring city-states under a pantheon of stars and gods. Their main achievements were intellectual, not political."

Only priests and the privileged held this knowledge, however, and they continued to develop it until the date-keeping and growth suddenly halted sometime after A.D. 800. By the end of that century, no buildings had been constructed, nor stelae erected.

Why were the centers abandoned? What happened to the priests and noblemen, the guardians of religion, science, and the arts? Theories abound. Some speculate social revolution; the people were tired of subservience and no longer willing to farm the land to provide food, clothing, and support for the priests and nobles. Other evidence points to population pressure on local resources combined with a series of devastating droughts. Whatever caused the great collapse (as it is known), most of the Maya's knowledge of astronomy, hieroglyphics, and architecture was not passed on to their Postclassic descendants.

COLONIALISM TO THE PRESENT

Though most major Maya population centers had collapsed 600 years before the arrival of the Spanish, many Maya survived, living in scattered pockets throughout the region. In 1519, 34-year-old Hernán Cortés sailed from Cuba searching for slaves; he began on the Yucatán coast and continued southward encountering the Maya. The Spanish believed Maya culture and religion was satanic and forcibly tried to exterminate both—even if this meant killing people in the process of saving souls. The Maya's resistance surprised Cortés, and fighting continued for many years with much bloodshed and death on both sides. Historians estimate that in the end, as many as 90 percent of the pre-conquest Maya population died from violence and from European diseases, including smallpox.

As the Maya world was divided up into colonial territories, and then into the independent nations of Mexico and Central America, the story of the indigenous people in each of these countries was largely parallel: Colonizers and *mestizos* (those of mixed European/indigenous descent) treated the Maya as landless, illiterate peasants with no right to property, or much of anything at all.

The situation erupted several times in rebellion, notably in a prolonged period of bloodshed and violence during the latter half of the 19th century in southern Mexico. The Yucatán Caste Wars, as this period is known, were fought in defense of communal Maya lands and over dignity and human rights. Despite these hardships, the Maya endured. Ronald Wright writes, "They abandoned some areas, lingered in others, migrated, merged, and adapted. They were and are eclectic: the Maya have always absorbed the culture of their conquerors and remade it as their own. They survived the Classic fall; and, better than any other Mesoamericans, they survived the Spanish invasion."

The Maya also survived state-sponsored terror and genocide in Guatemala in the latter part of the 20th century. The peace accord of 1995 finally ended the violence and allowed the Maya to practice their culture. Today, many Maya suffer widespread poverty in their communities, yet still continue to survive and thrive.

As ancient hieroglyphics become better understood, and as discoveries are made about Maya heritage, pride in Maya communities has increased, even while, in some areas, languages and customs are dying out faster than you can say "globalization."

The Maya Long Count

Maya hieroglyphics speak of stories, myths, events—and dates. The Maya shared a unique view of time, which they saw as a kind of infinite spiral staircase, as opposed to a simple linear notion. The celestial cycles they observed inspired a system of interlocking calendars of various lengths. Maya daykeepers, as their priests are known, built these cycles within a Long Count, or 5,125-year period of time, which began on August 11, 3114 B.C. The Long Count will end on December 21, 2012.

Within this span of time, any single day exists in the Long Count as a series of five numerical places:

1 *b'aktun* = 393 years (144,000 days)
1 *k'atun* = 20 years (7,200 days)
1 *tun* = 1 year (360 days)
1 *winal* = 20 days
1 *k'in* = 1 day

For example, 8.12.14.8.15 (written on Stela 29 in Tikal) is represented in two columns of glyphs and numbers, accompanied by cues that describe the date's significance. This numerical set translates as:

8 *b'aktuns*
12 *k'atuns*
14 *tuns*
8 *winals*
15 *k'ins*

These numbers give an exact measure of days after the start of the Long Count, correlating to July 8, A.D. 292, which is considered the beginning of the Classic Period. Entire books are dedicated to explaining the unique

DECIPHERING THE GLYPHS

For years, scholars could not agree whether the fantastic inscriptions found on Maya stelae, codices, and temple walls were anything more than complex records of numbers and dates. Many thought the text was not "real writing," as it did not appear to reproduce spoken language. Even those who believed the writing to be more meaningful despaired at ever reading it.

Mayanist and scholar Michael D. Coe's *Breaking the Maya Code* (New York: Thames and Hudson, 1992) is a fascinating account of the decipherment of Maya hieroglyphics. Coe describes how, in 1952, reclusive Russian scholar Yuri Valentinovich Knorosov made a crucial breakthrough by showing that Maya writing did in fact convey spoken words. Using a rough alphabet recorded by Fray Diego de Landa (the 16th-century bishop who, ironically, is best known for having destroyed numerous Maya texts), Knorosov showed that ancient texts contain common Yucatec Maya words such as *cutz* (turkey) and *tzul* (dog). Interestingly, Knorosov conducted his research from reproductions only, having never held a Maya artifact or visited an ancient temple. (When he did finally visit Tikal in 1990, Coe says Knorosov wasn't very impressed.)

But Knorosov's findings were met with staunch resistance by some of the field's most influential scholars, which delayed progress for decades. By the mid-1980s, however, decipherment picked up speed; one of many standouts from that era is David Stuart, the son of Maya experts, who went to Cobá with his parents at age eight and passed the time copying glyphs and learning Yucatec Maya words from local playmates. As a high school student he served as chief epigrapher on a groundbreaking exploration in Belize, and at age 18 he received a US$128,000 MacArthur Fellowship (aka "Genius Award") to, as he told Michael Coe, "play around with the glyphs" full-time.

Researchers now know that Maya writing is like most other hieroglyphic systems. What appears at first to be a single glyph can have up to four parts, and the same word can be expressed in pictorial, phonetic, or hybrid form. Depending on context, one symbol can have either a pictorial or phonetic role; likewise, a particular sound can be represented in more than one way. The word cacao is spelled phonetically as "ca-ca-u" but is written with a picture of a fish (*ca*) and a comb-like symbol (also *ca*, according to Landa) and followed by -u. One of David Stuart's great insights was that for all its complexity, much of Maya glyphic writing is "just repetitive."

But how do scholars know what the symbols are meant to sound like in the first place? Some come from the Landa alphabet, others are suggested by the pictures that accompany many texts, still others from patterns derived by linguistic analyses of contemporary Maya languages. In some cases, it is simply a hunch that, after applying it to a number of texts, turns out to be right. If this seems like somewhat shaky scientific ground, it is – but not without a means of being proved. The cacao decipherment was confirmed when the same glyph was found on a jar with cacao residue still inside.

Hundreds of glyphs have been deciphered, and most of the known Maya texts can be reliably translated. The effort has lent invaluable insight into Maya civilization, especially dynastic successions and religious beliefs. Some archaeologists lament, not unreasonably, that high-profile glyphic studies divert attention from research into the lives of everyday ancient Maya, who after all far outnumbered the nobility but are not at all represented in the inscriptions. That said, it's impossible not to marvel at how one of the world's great ancient civilizations is revealed in the whorls and creases of fading stone pictures.

– contributed by Liza Prado and Gary Chandler, authors of *Moon Cancún & Cozumel, Moon Yucatán Peninsula,* and *Moon Chiapas*

and complex base-20 Maya calendar system— Barbara Tedlock's *Time and the Highland Maya* is a standard on the subject.

Some believe that another cycle of 13 *b'aktuns* will begin when the old one ends and that the Long Count, much like a car odometer, will click over to 13.0.0.0.0 on December 21, 2012. Others consider this idea pure conjecture, and argue for an even longer count than five thousand years.

But if the purpose of the Long Count was not to pinpoint a transition at its end, then what was it? Dr. Edwin Barnhart writes about the Maya's "love of calculating the lowest common multiples and highest common divisors between the celestial cycles they were tracking." He says, "I believe the Long Count allowed them to tease those temporal conjunctions out and that they viewed them as the hidden synchronicities of the cosmos."

2012: THE MAYA PROPHECY

The beginnings and endings of cycles were big news for the Classic Maya—the bigger the cycle, the bigger the news. The *b'aktun* is an important unit, "used for describing the creations of humans and of the world," writes Gaspar Pedro González. Thirteen is a sacred number for the Maya as well, giving even more weight to the ending of the 13 *b'aktun* Long Count. The fact that the Maya pegged the end of the Long Count to the winter solstice is, for some, additional evidence of a prophecy or at least some intention by the ancient Maya.

Physical evidence of the Long Count (the 2012 date) is found inscribed on a monument at Tortuguero and in astronomy-based symbolism at Izapa and Copán. Some point to the Armageddon-like line in the *Popol Vuh*, the sacred Maya book, which reads, "It will rain fire, burning stones; the Earth will lift up; there will be floods that will put an end to humanity, to those who have vitiated the Earth." Even though these horrible events are not tied to 2012 in the *Popol Vuh*, it's still tantalizing stuff, especially for survivalists selling gas masks and custom bunkers.

Some simplify the 2012 prophecy debate as "believers vs. non-believers," or "those who think something will happen vs. those who don't." Academics and Maya scholars acknowledge that the Maya Long Count exists and does indeed end on December 21, 2012. But they scoff at the mention of asteroids, solar flares, extraterrestrials, or Planet X, to list a few popular doomsday theories.

After the 2011 Maya Meetings in Austin, Texas, which addressed the 2012 discussion, lecturer Dr. Robert Sitler reported that "the academic community has consistently described the international interest in the year 2012 and Mayan calendrics as a poorly informed product of misguided New Age ideologies with few substantive connections to the Mayan world." He continues, "Scholars are especially upset with extremist claims that 2012 will mark the end of the Mayan calendar and even the end of the world itself."

These thoughts are echoed in Mayanist scholar Mark Van Stone's book, *2012: Science and Prophecy of the Ancient Maya*. "There is nothing in the Maya or Aztec or ancient Mesoamerican prophecy," he writes, "to suggest that they prophesied a sudden or major change of any sort in 2012." He argues that 13 *b'aktuns* was nothing, and points to even longer counts at Palenque, including one indicating that 20 *b'aktuns* rather than 13 is the actual length of the Long Count. Another text at Palenque is inscribed with a date correlating to A.D. 4772. Van Stone says this proves that the people of Palenque not only expected to survive 13.0.0.0.0 (December 21, 2012), but to worship their kings and gods for thousands of years more.

"This is about the clearest message they gave us," Van Stone says, "that they (like us) could not imagine the End of their Culture, they expected it to live forever. Perhaps you could call this a static-cyclical conception of time. I call it normal human self-awareness."

THEORIES ABOUT 2012

Within the multi-disciplinary world of 2012ology, theories span the gamut from serious academic discussions of astronomical alignments by glyph-deciphering Maya geeks to theorists who think that, on December 21, 2012, the sun will cause a magnetic phenomenon triggering all human pineal glands to release a hallucinogen causing a mass humanity-wide transcendent trip. Other non-Maya–based theories predict Atlantis will rise, solar flares will explode, and extraterrestrials will return to Earth to beam away the chosen ones. (That last one is supposed to happen in the village of Bugarach, France. Seriously.)

The various branches and stems of 2012 studies are presented in hundreds of books and documentary films by academics, independent researchers, modern explorers, spiritualists, novelists, and curious armchair 2012 observers. This extensive field is made more intriguing (and confusing) by the wave of global rumor and hype that has carried the story. It has turned into a global meme, especially since the sensationalistic blockbuster film *2012* (released in 2009) soundly blasted the 2012 idea out of the hands of the Maya and into Hollywood and the mass media.

WHAT DO THE MAYA SAY?

For the most part, the Maya of today are too busy with day-to-day living to worry about the latest theory regarding 2012. Most grew up with no living reference to the Long Count or the ending of 13 *b'aktuns,* only learning about these things from outside archaeologists and epigraphers.

A friend who works in a small community in the Yucatán told me that the Maya of her village were "not particularly interested in nor do they care about the 2012 event." Other Maya are just as intrigued with the rediscovery of the Long Count and 2012 references as anyone else.

Still, too often the Maya themselves are left out of the 2012 discussion. As December 21, 2012, approaches, some communities in Mexico and Guatemala are taking matters into their own hands by sending delegations of Maya elders abroad to address global concerns about 2012. I attended one talk by a K'iche' elder in a community center outside Denver, Colorado, in 2011. He had come, he said, as a messenger from his grandfathers in the mountains of Guatemala with this message about 2012:

"A better world is possible! That is my *grano de maiz*" (my grain of corn), he said, "as we enter the age of the fifth sun." He told us about a school they were building in his village and of the ceremonies they were performing to prepare all of humanity for the upcoming transition.

"You are invited," he told the crowd of about 200 people. "The elders have opened the doors for whenever you'd like to come. Maya spirituality is for everyone. It is universal, it is not just for one group."

Dr. Jaime Awe, Director of Belize's Institute of Archaeology and part Maya himself, says that 2012 "represents the ending of one cosmological cycle, and the beginning of another. It's very much the way most people would look at the end of one year and the beginning of another, but over a very, very long period of time. It is a time for reflection, and for considering future direction."

Another Quiché elder, don Alejandro Cirilo Pérez Oxlaj, made this prediction: "With a new social order there comes a time of freedom where we can move like the clouds, without limitations, without borders. We will travel like the birds, without the need for passports. We will travel like the rivers, all heading towards the same point . . ."

Travel in 2012

MULTI-COUNTRY TOURS AND PACKAGES

It is entirely possible to piece together your own Maya-based adventure that ignores modern country boundaries. If you can afford the time and cost, independent travel is a great way to go, as long as you can devote a minimum of a few days to each country and avoid day trips to Tikal from Belize or other rush jobs at world-class sites. Be careful of spreading yourself too thin with your limited time.

Multi-country tours allow travelers to note subtle cultural differences as they pass between Honduras and Guatemala, or between Central America and Mexico—or between anywhere and Belize. If you'd rather leave the planning to someone else, explore one of the following 2012-related tours offered by a range of experts.

Archaeological Tours

The highly experienced and knowledgeable guides at Archaeological Tours (tel. 212/986-3054 or 866/740-5130, www.archaeologicaltrs.com) have been giving professional tours of the Mundo Maya for a long time. They have two trips planned in 2012: **Lords of the River and the Plains: The Northern Maya Kingdoms** (16 days, Jan. 6–21, 2012, approx. US$5,500 per person) and **Guatemala with Copán** (15 days, Mar. 3–17, 2012, approx. US$4,700). Both are led by William Saturno, a professor of anthropology at Boston University. Dr. Saturno received his PhD at Harvard University and has conducted research throughout all the Mundo Maya countries.

Maya Exploration Center

The Maya Exploration Center (MEC, www.mayaexploration.org) is a nonprofit organization based in Austin, Texas, dedicated to the study of ancient Maya civilization. They offer regular courses for travelers, a lecture series, and education programs for students, teachers, and the general public. On MEC trips, the fee covers lodging, transportation, entry fees,

© JOSHUA BERMAN

village fiesta in Mexico

breakfasts, archaeological guides, five evening lectures, and a final dinner. They have two special trips planned for 2012.

Ancient Calendars and Modern Maya: Summer Solstice 2012 Tour (June 19–29, 2012, $2,800 per person) is led by archaeologist Dr. Christopher Powell. The trip begins in Villahermosa and travels to Chiapas, Mexico, and the highlands of Guatemala. It starts with a doozy: a private viewing of Tortuguero Monument 6 (the only stela in the Maya world with the date December 21, 2012). Next is summer solstice at Palenque, where you'll get to see the dawn hierophany (trick of light and shadow) in the Temple of the Sun. This is followed by a boat trip up the Río Usumacinta to view the "deep time" date panel at Yaxchilán, followed by the Maya village of Chamula for their biggest festival of the year. The trip continues on to Izapa, where the Long Count may have began, and Lake Atitlán, Guatemala.

Another 2012 MEC offering is **Surfing the Zenith in the Maya World: Zenith Passage 2012 Tour** (8 days, Aug. 5–15, 2012, $3,100 per person). The trip begins in Guatemala City, where your guide, archaeologist Dr. Edwin Barnhart, will give an introductory lecture followed by a museum visit. An afternoon flight to Flores in the Petén leads to Tikal and a boat trip up the Río Pasión to Ceibal for the first zenith passage. The tour chases the zenith passage south to witness it again in Quiriguá, where the tallest stela in the Maya world stands. Afterwards the tour travels to Copán for the zenith passage on the Maya creation anniversary of August 13. The tour stays in Copán for two days before finishing in Guatemala City with a visit to the National Anthropology Museum and a celebratory final dinner.

Maya Field Workshops

Maya Field Workshops (www.mayafieldworkshops.com, mayafieldworkshops@gmail.com) conducts intensive on-site seminars on Maya studies. Renowned archaeologist and epigrapher Dr. David Stuart will be offering two workshops in 2012: one in Copán during the second week in June, and the other in Palenque the second week of December.

Mayan Traveler

The Mayan Traveler (tel. 888/843-6292 or 713-299-5665, www.themayantraveler.com) is a long-established Maya tour specialist. Their 2012 offerings will satisfy the most serious temple junkies. Sign up for the seven-night **Maya Adventure Tour,** which includes the top sites of Honduras, Guatemala, and Belize with visits to Copán, Quiriguá, Xunantunich, Yaxhá, Caracol, Tikal, and Ceibal. Tours begin on the first and third Saturdays of each month and begin and end in Guatemala City.

The **Best of the Maya** Tour begins in Villahermosa, Mexico, and continues to Guatemala before ending in Honduras. Guests will meet some of the region's top archaeologists along the way, including Dr. Ed Barnhardt, Christopher Powell, and David Sedat, who lecture and answer questions at key sites.

The **Ancient and Living Maya in 2012** trip focuses on some of the most important sites in Maya calendar development. The tour begins in Antigua then presses on to Izapa, Mexico, the birthplace of the Long Count. This is followed by a night in Tapachula before returning to Guatemala and the Preclassic jewel of Tak'alik Ab'aj, the market of Chichicastenango, Tikal, Yaxhá, and two sites in Belize. They have even longer trips, including a 10-night **Great Cities of the Maya** covering Copán, Quiriguá, Xunantunich, Yaxhá, Caracol, Tikal, Bonampak, Yaxchilán, Piedras Negras, Sak-Tzi, Palenque, and Tonina. Whew.

MayaSites Travel

MayaSites Travel (tel. 877/620-8715, mayasites@yahoo.com, www.mayasites.com) is offering various **Traveling in Maya Time** tours in Mexico and Guatemala over the 2012 winter solstice. They also do custom trips.

Viaventure

Antigua-based Viaventure (tel. 502/7832-2509, marcia.vanog@viaventure.com, www.viaventure.com) is a full-service tour operator specializing in Guatemala, Belize, and Honduras. They offer a number of five-day tours in each country (available year-round outside peak seasons), plus custom trips. In 2012, they are adding a 12-day **Maya Magic and Mystery** tour. It begins in Antigua, Guatemala, with tours of the area and a workshop on jade and fair-trade coffee. Guests continue through the lake area on more coffee tours, boat rides, and a visit to the Chichicastenango Market. Sign up to see a shaman ritual at Pascal Abaj as well. After that, you're off to Copán and the Petén.

MAYA FOUNDATIONS
Casa Herrera

Casa Herrera (www.utmesoamerica.org) is a research, conference, and teaching facility in Antigua, Guatemala. It acts as an extension of the Mesoamerica Center of the University of Texas at Austin's Department of Art and Art History. They promote the study of pre-Columbian art, archaeology, history, and culture through education and research, and will be hosting the 2012 Maya Meetings in March, 2012.

Foundation for the Advancement of Mesoamerican Studies

The Foundation for the Advancement of Mesoamerican Studies (FAMSI, www.famsi. org) was created in 1993 to increase the world's understanding of ancient Mesoamerican cultures. The organization assists researchers and maintains an email list called AZTLAN for like-minded Mayaphiles. The list is "open to all persons interested in pre-Columbian cultures, whether amateurs or professionals."

Institute of Maya Studies

The mission of the Institute of Maya Studies (IMS, www.instituteofmayastudies.org) is "to help spread knowledge on the pre-Columbian cultures of the Americas," with an emphasis on the Maya. The IMS was founded in 1971 and is affiliated with the Miami Science Museum.

Maya Conservancy

The Maya Conservancy (info@mayaconservancy.org, www.mayaconservancy.org) is based in Austin, Texas, and works to preserve and protect Maya and pre-Maya archaeological

sites throughout Central America. Their projects include improving the restoration and accessibility of the Izapa archaeological zone in Mexico.

Saq' Be'

Saq' Be' (www.sacredroad.org) is a nonprofit organization formed in the United States and named after "the sacred white road." Trips are led by Ajq'ij (Maya priest) and the Organization for Mayan and Indigenous Spiritual Studies. They aim to teach the public about current indigenous struggles, assist indigenous communities, and arrange for meetings and exchanges between spiritual leaders of various indigenous communities.

VOLUNTEER OPPORTUNITIES

One sure-fire way to prepare for the new Age of Man is to roll up your sleeves and jump on the "voluntourism" bandwagon, combining service work with your travels. You have to be careful and qualified; you don't want to be more hindrance than help, nor do you want to demean anyone or create dependency. One past participant in a Yucatán voluntourism project explained it this way: "The concept is that volunteers often come thinking that they will 'help the poor Maya' and leave realizing that the opposite was true: The cultural exchange taught them about life, family, and community."

What do you have to offer? What do you want to learn?

Resources

Voluntourism guru Nola Lee Kelsey's collection of alternative travel opportunities, **700 Places to Volunteer Before You Die: A Traveler's Guide** is an excellent place to begin, listing numerous organizations in the Mundo Maya countries and beyond (it also includes tips from yours truly and others on how to select a program). Sign up to the author's "V-List" to stay updated.

Another important tool are the country search boxes at either **www.go-volunteerabroad. com** or **www.volunteerabroad.com**, which maintain long, updated lists of alternative travel and service opportunities.

Organizations

The tour schedule at **Sustainable Harvest International**'s Build a Smaller World program (tel. 408/384-8376, www.sustainable-harvest.org/travel) offers community-based, service-learning experiences in various Mundo Maya countries. In southern Belize, they help travelers (individuals, groups, and families)

who are staying at Cotton Tree Lodge book volunteer projects in the area.

"To heal the world" is the mission of **American Jewish World Service** (www.ajws.org), one international development organization that supports many community projects across the Mundo Maya with small grants. They also offer volunteer opportunities in the spring and summer throughout the region for qualified applicants of various age groups.

Resources

SUGGESTED READING 2012

Hundreds of books have been written about the Maya calendar and the end of the Long Count. Here are just a few suggested titles that offer an overview of the 2012 phenomenon from a few different perspectives.

González, Gaspar Pedro. *13 B'aktun: Mayan Visions of 2012 and Beyond.* Berkeley, CA: North Atlantic Books, 2010. Unlike any other book you'll read about 2012, this one was written in Spanish by a Maya novelist and philosopher from Guatemala then translated to English. The book is comprised of a lyrical dialogue, poetry, explanations of Maya concepts, messages to the West, and more. The author writes, "if on Earth we haven't been able to become conscientious about nature, our mission, and our relationship with the other beings that exist here, we won't be able to attain cosmic, more distant, and more spiritual consciousness as humans."

Jenkins, John Major. *The 2012 Story: The Myths, Fallacies, and Truth Behind the Most Intriguing Date in History.* New York: Tarcher/Penguin, 2009. If you are only going to read one book on 2012—or if you are looking for a far-reaching portal to the greater 2012 world, this is the book. Jenkins is one of the most prolific and passionate 2012ologists out there. His 1998

book *Maya Cosmogenesis 2012* is regarded as a groundbreaking work in the field, "easily one of the best researched of the popular books that focus on the 2012 date," writes one colleague. In *The 2012 Story,* Jenkins covers everything from the ancients' forward-reaching stone inscriptions to 2012 as a modern global meme. He writes, "2012 has gained the status of an icon, a cultural symbol, to be used and often abused for purposes that have nothing to do with its origins and the intentions of its creators." The book sums up Jenkins's galactic alignment theory and others' work as well.

Sitler, Robert, PhD. *The Living Maya: Ancient Wisdom in the Era of 2012.* Berkeley, CA: North Atlantic Books, 2010. This book begins with the Yucatec Maya greeting, "Bix a bel?," which means, "How is your road?" And that's right where the author puts us—on the road in the Guatemalan highlands and southern Mexico, traveling with him in the forest. Some of his anecdotes and encounters happened long before he became a professor at Stetson University in DeLand, Florida; others are based on his three decades of working with the Maya. The book weaves these narratives with cultural explanations and lessons we can learn from the Maya of today.

Stuart, David. *The Order of Days: The Maya World and the Truth About Maya Time.* New

York: Random House, 2011. Esteemed epigrapher and author of half a dozen books on Maya hieroglyphics and archaeology, Dr. David Stuart is one of the world's most preeminent Mayanists. In his newest book, he explains the science behind the 2012 speculations.

Van Stone, Mark. *2012: Science and Prophecy of the Ancient Maya*. San Diego: Tlacaélel Press, 2010. This book is a science-based skeptic's guide to the subject, written by a respected Mayanist, epigrapher, and professional art historian. This remarkable book is overflowing with color illustrations, glyph descriptions, date breakdowns, and a very thorough investigation of the various 2012 theories.

The Maya

Arvigo, Rosita. *Sastun: One Woman's Apprenticeship with a Maya Healer and Their Efforts to Save the Vani*. San Francisco: Harper, 1995. *Sastun* tells the story of the American-born author's training with 87-year-old Elijio Panti, the best-known Maya medicine man in Central America. It takes place in the remote, roadless expanse of Cayo District in western Belize.

Coe, Michael D. *The Maya* (8th ed.). New York: Thames & Hudson, 2011. Coe, an archaeologist, anthropologist, epigrapher, and author, is a forefather of Maya studies, and this book is mandatory reading for both amateur Mayanists and pros. He attempts to understand the "most intellectually sophisticated and aesthetically refined pre-Columbian culture," as Coe calls the Maya. *The Maya* has been in print for nearly 50 years and is a classic, easy-to-read text, for consumption either at home before you go, or packed along as a field guide. The eighth edition has information on recent discoveries, including the polychrome murals of Calakmul, and increased evidence of Preclassic sophistication.

De Landa, Friar Diego. *Yucatán: Before and After the Conquest*. New York: Dover

Publications, 1978 (translation of original manuscript written in 1566). The same man who provided some of the best, most lasting descriptions of ancient Maya also single-handedly destroyed more Maya artifacts and writings than anyone in history. Yet this book has provided crucial clues to modern understanding of the Maya and their calendar and writing.

Tedlock, Barbara, PhD. *Time and the Highland Maya*. Albuquerque: University of New Mexico Press, 1982, 1992. This is the classic primer on understanding the complex system of Maya calendars and their meaning to the Maya of Guatemala's western highlands. A professor of anthropology at the University of Buffalo, Tedlock is an expert in Maya calendrical divination and was trained with her husband as a daykeeper and spiritual diviner by shamans in Momostenango, Guatemala.

Travel Narratives

Fry, Joan. *How to Cook a Tapir: A Memoir of Belize*. Lincoln: University of Nebraska Press, 2009. The story of a young teacher's year abroad, living among the Maya in southern Belize nearly 50 years ago. The author offers an intimate glimpse at Maya village life in this heartfelt, oftentimes funny story of how she "painstakingly baked and boiled her way up the food chain" to gain acceptance among her neighbors and students.

Kelsey, Nola Lee. *700 Places to Volunteer Before You Die: A Traveler's Guide*. Hot Springs, SD: Dog's Eye View Media, 2010. A fine collection of alternative travel opportunities in the Mundo Maya countries and beyond.

McConahay, Mary Jo. *Maya Roads: One Woman's Journey Among the People of the Rainforest*. Chicago: Chicago Review Press, 2011. After three decades traveling and working in some of the remotest corners of the Mundo Maya, the author, an award-winning television producer, has written a wonderful, lyrical travelogue. While moving through thick forests and down wide rivers, McConahay gives the reader a front row seat to archaeological discoveries, the transformation of the Lacandón people, the Zapatista indigenous uprising in Chiapas, and uncovering a war crime in Guatemala.

Stephens, John Lloyd. *Incidents of Travel in Central America, Chiapas and Yucatán.* New York: Dover Publications, Inc., 1969 (New York: originally Harper & Bros., 1841). A smashing 19th-century travelogue, Stephens's writing is wonderfully pompous, amusing, and astute—with historical and archaeological observations that still stand today. If you can, find a copy with the original set of illustrations by Stephens's expedition partner and artist, Frederick Catherwood.

Wright, Ronald. *Time Among the Maya: Travels in Belize, Guatemala, and Mexico.* New York: Grove Press, 2000. This narrative carries the reader through the Mundo Maya countries on a series of encounters and visits during some of the tenser recent decades. Wright paints vivid scenes and does not shy away from difficult subjects. "Tourism exploits the Indian, but the Indian suffers when tourism is withdrawn. The dilemma is one of control, and it will remain unresolved until the larger question of Indian rights in Guatemala is addressed," he writes.

Travel Guides

Argueta, Al. *Moon Guatemala.* Berkeley, CA: Avalon Travel, 2010.

Berman, Joshua. *Moon Belize.* Berkeley, CA: Avalon Travel, 2011.

Chandler, Gary, and Liza Prado. *Moon Cancún & Cozumel* (2011), *Moon Chiapas* (2009), and *Moon Yucatán Peninsula* (2011). Berkeley, CA: Avalon Travel.

Robertson, Amy E., and Christopher Humphrey. *Moon Honduras & the Bay Islands.* Berkeley, CA: Avalon Travel, 2009.

SUGGESTED VIEWING

2012: The True Mayan Prophecy (ww.2012 thetruemayanprophecy.com). This thoughtful independent film by Dawn Engle was an undertaking of the Peace Jam Foundation, an organization based in Denver, Colorado, that connects Nobel laureates with students. Excitement over 2012, and the current period of "disordered time" (which was predicted to last from 1992 to 2032, we learn), are used as an opening for Nobel Peace Prize winner and Guatemalan human rights advocate Rigoberta Menchú and a council of Maya elders to offer viewers a Maya perspective: "Our sacred Mayan calendar is acquiring an extraordinary importance for the planet," says Menchu before offering positive courses of action that we can follow. She is joined by no less than the Dalai Lama and Bishop Desmond Tutu, who also talk about ways out of the current period of hate, violence, and negativity.

Apocalypto (2006). This film is not about 2012, but it suggests a metaphor between current chaos and the collapse of the Classic Maya period, when this film takes place. Producer Mel Gibson spent $40 million to visually re-create the ancient Maya world, where this action-adventure-drama is set. It was filmed in Mexico, at Catemaco, San Andrés Tuxtla, and Paso de Ovejas in Veracruz. The viewer races through the forest with Jaguar Paw, a young Maya captured for sacrifice who is trying to save his family. Along the way, we see a brutal, gory snapshot of an empire in decline. Critics call it inaccurate and even racist, the old "brutal savage" stereotype that reflects badly on modern Maya. Although there are several historical and archaeological inaccuracies (or liberties), the film gets many details right, especially the language—the whole film is in spoken Yucatec Mayan from that age, reconstructed by linguists and archaeologists. If you'd rather skip the bloody, heart-wrenching (literally) parts of *Apocalypto,* you should still watch the first 10 minutes for a glimpse of idyllic Maya village life.

Cracking the Maya Code (2004). Everything by NOVA on the Maya is worth watching. This fascinating hour-long documentary, based on Michael Coe's 1999 book *Breaking the Maya Code,* "chronicles the 200-year worldwide quest by linguists, mathematicians, artists, architects, archaeologists, and others to decipher the Maya hieroglyphs." It focuses on the Maya's system of glyphs, explaining their meaning as both symbols and phonetic sounds.

Dawn of the Maya (2008). This National Geographic documentary tells about recent breakthroughs in scientists' thoughts on the Preclassic Maya. It focuses on discoveries made at El Mirador, in far northern Guatemala, and also Palenque.

INTERNET RESOURCES

I found surprisingly few helpful, fun, or even well-designed 2012-specific websites during my research. A few forums appeared to have been started with good intentions but were taken over by survivalists comparing guns and bunker designs. Here are some important portal-type sites to begin your studies. Consult the country travel planners and my 2012 Travel Blog on www.moon.com.

2012
www.alignment2012.com
The website of John Major Jenkins, an independent researcher devoted to reconstructing ancient Mayan cosmology and philosophy.

www.diagnosis2012.co.uk
This comprehensive database (aka "Dire Gnosis") on all things 2012 is kept by author Geoff Stray, who continually updates it with new videos, articles, and 2012 news.

Mexico
www.yucatan.travel

Guatemala
www.pueblosmayas.com
www.2012guatemala.com

Belize
www.belizemaya2012.com

Honduras
www.letsgohonduras.com

Maya Calendar
www.mayan-calendar.com
Created by archaeologist Dr. Edwin Barnhart, this site is an accurate date converter and home to the Maya Calendar smartphone app, which can convert Long Count dates and birthdays without an Internet connection (perfect for when you're at a remote Maya site, making a groundbreaking discovery).

www.maya-portal.net
The Mayan Calendar Portal is a vast source of Maya calendar information, offering a *tzolk'in* birthday calculator app, daily energy readings, webinars, Meet the Artist/Author events, and blogs by various personalities working in the Maya world, including elder Don Rigoberto Itzep Chanchavac.

Maya Studies
www.famsi.org
The Foundation for the Advancement of Mesoamerican Studies is an excellent resource for news on Mundo Maya discoveries and ongoing research.

www.mesoweb.com
This "exploration of Mesoamerican cultures" is a fantastic portal to the world of Maya studies, maintained by some of the top archaeologists and experts in the field.

Q&A: BARBARA MACLEOD, PHD, ANTHROPOLOGIST

When a major Hollywood producer is making a period piece set in ancient Maya times and wants the actors to learn and use authentic ancient Yucatec Mayan speech, he calls Barb Mac Leod, PhD, anthropologist, Mayan language and hieroglyphic writing expert, stunt pilot, and Returned Peace Corps Volunteer (she helped explore and map the caves of Belize as part of her assignment in the early 1970s). Her work is heard throughout the film *Apocalypto*, which races through a Terminal Classic Maya world at breakneck speed. "It was a blitz of long days in the studio," says Dr. MacLeod. "My role was to help the actors with proper pronunciation during post-production, when audio was added or replaced. Mel Gibson was very much on top of every detail; I liked that."

When did you first travel to a country in the Mundo Maya? Where did you go and how did it impact you?
It was my first trip to Belize, in the summer of 1970. I went there to explore caves. We had been corresponding with an American geologist who lived there and who had visited a number of caves. It was amazing; it turned my life around. The caving was excellent. I also visited Palenque on this trip, which blew me away.

How difficult was it to learn Mayan? How many Mayan languages can you speak?
It wasn't difficult for me; I have a knack for languages and am a grammar nut. I only speak one Mayan language, Yucatec (but I'm rusty), but I know the grammar of 10 languages and can read their texts without difficulty.

How is the Mayan language distinct when compared to other world languages? What most sets it apart?
Glad you asked: ergative-absolutive case marking and glottalized consonants. Other Native American languages have the latter.

What does "responsible tourism" mean when traveling in the Mundo Maya?
This is a complex issue. It's important to segregate visits by tourists to Maya sites which are set up for tourism from visits to indigenous communities which are (for the most part) not prepared for tourism, except on a small scale or by invitation. It goes without saying that visitors must be respectful at many levels. It is also important to find ways to give something back to the Maya people who are visited – and by this I don't mean tips and gratuities, though those might be appropriate. Some archaeology tour companies have programs whereby a portion of the fee is donated to a community project – housing, school, clinics. People traveling in groups are better able to elicit suggestions from community elders and make donations. But we need to consider other things to donate besides money. Workshops for local people in

© CJ RUSHIN

MacLeod (left with clipboard) maps Maya artifacts in Uch'en Kimen cave, Belize.

archaeology and Maya writing have been very successful in Guatemala.

Do you have any travel plans in the year 2012

I am sure there will be events at major cities like Tikal and Palenque. I don't have my finger on the pulse, and would myself stay away; I don't usually like big crowds. I did celebrate the 12.18.0.0.0 *k'atun* ending in July 1973 at Tikal. By myself – no one else was interested. I was living in Belize at the time, so it was an easy trip. Should people visit a main temple on this date? Sure! I am all for this being a grand party, even if I'm the one who'd prefer to be off in a quiet room.

YUCATEC MAYAN GLOSSARY

Yucatec Maya is spoken by around 800,000 people, and is the most commonly spoken Maya language in the Yucatán Peninsula (and second overall, after K'iche in Guatemala). It is also spoken by many Maya in central and northern Belize. Most ancient glyphs were written in early forms of Yucatec Maya or another Maya language, Ch'ol.

Maya Gods and Ceremonies

Acanum protective deity of hunters

Ahau Can serpent lord and highest priest

Ahau Chamehes deity of medicine

Ah Cantzicnal aquatic deity

Ah Chuy Kak god of violent death and sacrifice

Ahcit Dzamalcum protective god of fishermen

Ah Cup Cacap god of the underworld who denies air

Ah Itzám the water witch

Ah kines priests who consult the oracles and preside over ceremonies and sacrifices

Ahpua god of fishing

Ah Puch god of death

Ak'Al sacred marsh where water abounds

Bacaboob supporters of the sky and guardians of the cardinal points, who form a single god, Ah Cantzicnal Becabs

Bolontiku the nine lords of the night

Chaac god of rain and agriculture

Chac Bolay Can butcher serpent living in the underworld

Chaces priests' assistants in agricultural and other ceremonies

Cihuateteo women who become goddesses through death in childbirth

Cit Chac Coh god of war

Hetzmek ceremony when the child is first carried astride the hip

Hobnil Bacab bee god, protector of beekeepers

Holcanes warriors charged with obtaining slaves for sacrifice

Hunab Ku giver of life, builder of the universe, and father of Itzámna

Ik god of the wind

Itzámna lord of the skies, creator of the beginning, god of time

Ixchel goddess of birth, fertility, and medicine; credited with inventing spinning

Ixtab goddess of the cord and of suicide by hanging

Kinich face of the sun

Kukulcán quetzal-serpent, plumed serpent

Metnal the underworld, place of the dead

Nacom warrior chief

Noh Ek Venus

Pakat god of violent death

Zec spirit lords of beehives

Food and Drink

alche inebriating drink, sweetened with honey and used for ceremonies and offerings

ic chili

itz sweet potato

kabaxbuul heaviest meal of the day, eaten at dusk and containing cooked black beans

kah pinole flour

kayem ground maize

macal a root

muxubbak tamale

on avocado

op plum

p'ac tomatoes

put papaya

tzamna black bean

uah tortillas

za maize drink

Animals

acehpek dog used for deer hunting

ah maax cal prattling monkey

ah maycuy chestnut deer

ah sac dziu white thrush

ah xixteel ul rugged land conch

bil hairless dog reared for food

cutz wild turkey

cutzha duck

hoh crow

icim owl

jaleb hairless dog

keh deer

kitam wild boar

muan evil bird related to death

que parrot

thul rabbit

tzo domestic turkey

utiu coyote

Music and Festivals

ah paxboob musicians

bexelac turtle shell used as percussion instrument

chohom dance performed in ceremonies related to fishing

chul flute

hom trumpet

kayab percussion instrument fashioned from turtle shell

Oc na festival where old idols of a temple are broken and replaced with new ones

okot uil dance performed during the Pocan ceremony

Pacum chac festival in honor of the war gods

tunkul drum

zacatan drum made from a hollowed tree trunk; one opening is covered with hide

Elements of Time

baktun 144,000-day Maya calendar

chumuc akab midnight

chumuc kin midday

emelkin sunset

haab solar calendar of 360 days plus five extra days of misfortune, which complete the final month

kaz akab dusk

kin the sun, the day, the unity of time

potakab time before dawn

yalhalcab dawn

Numbers

hun one

ca two

ox three

can four

ho five

uac six

uuc seven

uacax eight

bolon nine

iahun 10

buluc 11

iahca 12

oxlahum 13

canlahum 14

holahun 15

uaclahun 16

uuclahun 17

uacaclahun 18

bolontahun 19

hunkal 20

Plants and Trees

ha cacao seed

kan ak plant that produces a yellow dye

ki sisal

kiixpaxhkum chayote

kikche tree trunk that is used to make canoes

kuche red cedar tree

k'uxub annatto tree

piim fiber of the cotton tree

taman cotton plant

tauch black zapote tree

tazon te moss

Miscellaneous Words

ah kay kin bak meat-seller

chaltun water cistern

cha te black vegetable dye

chi te eugenia, plant for dyeing

ch'oh indigo

ek dye

hadzab wooden swords

halach uinic leader

mayacimil smallpox epidemic

palapa traditional Maya structure constructed without nails or tools

pic underskirt

ploms rich people

suyen square blanket

xanab sandals

xicul sleeveless jacket decorated with feathers

xul stake with a pointed, fire-hardened tip

yuntun slings

Courtesy of Liza Prado and Gary Chandler, authors of *Moon Cancún & Cozumel, Moon Yucatán Peninsula,* and *Moon Chiapas.*

TZOTZIL MAYAN GLOSSARY

Tzotzil is one of the most widely used Maya languages in Chiapas, Mexico, spoken by over 35 percent of the state's indigenous population.

ac'ubal night
atimol bathroom
avocoluc please
bat me good-bye
bats'i c'obil right (directional)
be walking path
beq'uet meat
biil name
ca' horse
c'ac'al day; sun
c'a'ep trash
cajvel coffee
canava boat
caxlan chicken
caxlan-c'op Spanish
chenec' bean
chij sheep
ch'ilbil fried
chitom pig
ch'ivit town plaza
chon animal
chopol bad
chotlebal seat
choy fish
chucvanab jail or prison
ch'ulna church
c'oc' fever; hot (temperature)
colaval thank you
c'u'il clothes
c'uxi hello
c'u yepal how much
jabnaltic forest
jamal open
jbeiltasvanej guide
jcaxlan person of mixed European and indigenous descent
jch'ulme'tic moon
j'ilvanej indigenous medicine man or woman
jo' water; rain
jolob a weaving
jpoxtavanej doctor
jteclum town or people
juch'bil chichol hot sauce
jxcanvil passenger
ich chili pepper, sometimes hot sauce
ixim corn
lec good
lobajel fruit
loc'ol photograph
luch embroidery
macal closed
mal c'ac'al afternoon
mayol municipal police
moch basket of woven reeds, with handle
mo'oj no
muc' ta jteclum city
muc'tic jabnaltic jungle
mut bird
na house
nab lake
natil c'u'il huipil, traditional Maya woman's embroidered shirt
oc'ob morning
pinca farm
pop a mat, traditionally woven of palm leaf
pus temazcal, Maya steam bath
q'uin party
Riox God
schi'il friend
sc'uxul pain
sic cold
syaveal door key
ta moton free
tana yes
tan-us "no-see-um" biting gnat
ta slajes to eat
ta x'ac'otaj to dance
ta xanav to walk
te' tree
tem bed
t'ot' literally, a snail; in the Maya world, it represents the cycle of life and death; in Zapatista speak, an administrative center or village
tsa'nel diarrhea
ts'omol left (directional)
ts'ib bolom jaguar
ts'omol bank
ts'unbaltic garden
tuch'ich' early 1800s-style horse-drawn carriage
tulix cigarette

uch'omo popular *pozole* stew of hominy in broth, usually topped by shredded pork, cabbage, and diced onion

uc'um river

us mosquito

vaj tortilla

ve'el ta mal c'ac'al dinner

ve'lil food

ve'lil ta sob breakfast

vinic man

xavon soap

xemana week

ya spicy

yajval jteclum indigenous or aboriginal inhabitant of all-native descent who speaks his or her native tongue

yaxte' ceiba tree or giant silk-cotton tree; in the Maya world, a sacred tree connecting the Earth to the upper and lower realms

Tzotzil Maya Glossary adapted from *Diccionario Tzotzil de San Andrés.* Hidalgo, Mexico: Summer Institute of Linguistics, 1986. Used with permission by Gary Chandler and Liza Prado, authors of *Moon Cancún & Cozumel, Moon Yucatán Peninsula,* and *Moon Chiapas.*

Q'EQCHI' MAYAN PHRASEBOOK

Most of southern Belize's people of indigenous descent speak Q'eqchi' Maya—though some communities speak the Mopan language instead, which is more closely related to Yucatec or Itzá Maya.

In Belize, you may see the word Q'eqchi' spelled different ways. "Kekchi" is how Protestant missionaries labeled the Maya of southern Belize, and British colonial officials wrote "Ketchi." Today, in neighboring Guatemala, the indigenous leaders of the Guatemalan Academy of Maya Languages (ALMG) have developed a standard Maya alphabet that the Q'eqchi' leaders in Belize have begun to use as well.

Making even a small attempt to speak and learn the language of your Maya hosts will deepen your experience. Never mind the laughs your funny accent will attract—your

---

HAPPY TRAILS: SAY IT IN MAYAN

Xi'ik tech utzil: "That you go well" (Yucatec Mayan)

Bix a bel?: "How is your road?" (Yucatec Mayan)

Ta'quil a'quib: "Safe travels" (Q'eqchi' Mayan)

Ta na cuente uee: "That you go well" (Quiché Mayan)

Timil timil sa' b'e: "Go slowly on the road" (Q'eqchi' Mayan)

Chaawil aawib': "Take care" (Q'eqchi' Mayan)

Che yil heb'a: "That you go well" (Q'anjob'al Mayan)

Que le vaya bien: "That you go well" (Spanish)

---

noble attempts are an amusing novelty, and no one means any harm. Persist, and you will be rewarded in ways you would never have expected—indeed, learning another language in such an immersing setting is one of the most humbling and empowering experiences a traveler can have.

Should you want to learn more than the few words presented here, track down the grammar book and cassette tapes by Q'eqchi' linguist Rigoberto Baq, available in Guatemala City at the Academia de Lenguas Mayas (www.almg.org.gt) or at their regional offices in Coban, Alta Verapaz (in the municipal palace), or Poptán, Petén.

Basic Phrases

All Q'eqchi' words have an accent on the last syllable. One of the first things you will probably be asked is, *"B'ar xat chalk chaq?"* (bar shaht chalk chok), to which you can respond, *"Xin chalk chaq sa'* New York" (sheen chalk chok sah New York, or wherever you are from).

In Q'eqchi', there are no words for "good morning," "good afternoon," or "good evening." You simply use the standard greeting, *"Ma sa sa' laa ch'ool"* (mah sah sah laa ch'ohl), literally, "Is there happiness in your heart?" (In Q'eqchi', however, you wouldn't use a question mark because the *"Ma"* indicates a question.) A proper response would be *"Sa in ch'ool"* (sah een ch'ohl), "Yes, my heart is happy."

Although it is falling out of custom with the younger generation, if you are speaking with an older woman or man, she or he would be delighted to be greeted with the terms of respect for the elderly: *"Nachin"* (nah cheen) for an elder woman, and *"Wachin"* (kwah cheen) for an elder man.

If you decide to go swimming in one of Toledo's beautiful rivers, you might want to ask first, *"Ma wan li ahin sa' li nima'"* (mah kwan lee aheen sa li neemah), which means, "Are there crocodiles in the river?"

"Ani laa kab'a?" (anee lah kabah) means "What's your name?" You can respond: *"Ix* (eesh) WOMAN'S NAME *in kab'a* (een kabah)" or *"Laj* MAN'S NAME *in kab'a* (een kabah)."

More Phrases and Vocabulary

Chan xaawil? (chan shaa kwil) What's up?
Jo xaqa'in (hoe shakaeen) Not much, just fine.
B'an usilal (ban ooseelal) Please.
B'antiox (ban teeosh) or *T'ho-kre (ta-HOH cree)* Thank you.
Us (oos) Good
Yib' i ru (yeeb ee rue) bad, ugly
Hehe (eheh) yes
Ink'a (eenk'ah) no
K'aru? (kaieeroo) What?
B'ar? (bar) Where?

Joq'e? (hoekay) When?
Jarub'? (hahrueb) How many?
Jonimal tzaq? (hoeneemahl ssahq) How much does it cost?
Chaawil aawib (chah kwil aakweeb) Take care of yourself (a good way to say goodbye).
Jowan chik (hoekwan cheek) See you later.
Wi chik (kwee cheek) again
wa (kwah) tortilla
kenq (kenk) beans
molb' (mohlb') eggs
kaxlan wa (kashlan kwah) bread
tib' (cheeb) meat
tzilan (sseeelan) chicken
kuy (kue-ee) pork/pig
kar (car) fish
chin (cheen) orange
kakaw (cacao) chocolate
ha' (hah) water
woqxinb'il ha' (kwohk sheen bill hah) boiled water
cape (kahpay) coffee
sulul (suelul) mud
ab' (ahb) hammock
chaat (chaht) bed
nima' (neemah) river
kokal (kohkahl) children
chaab'il (chahbill) good
kaw (kauw) hard
najt (nahjt) far
nach (nahch) close

(Special thanks to Clark University anthropologist Liza Grandia, PhD, who spent four years among the Maya.)

Index

List of Maps

Son, have no fear, What you see is everyone running to the highest point in the Cuchumatans, the tallest mountain range in Central America, to witness the phenomenon of the winter solstice. Look, they're coming from all parts of the world. The light we see is the reflection of the ceremonial fires of the ajtxajs [spiritual guides]. There are immense bonfires celebrating the new day. The aurora is coming, the dawn is coming, the light of the New Era.

—Gaspar Pedro González

Acknowledgments

This book's origins date to 3114 B.C. when the Long Count began—or at least as far back as Mick and Lucy Fleming's A.D. 2010 Christmas caroling party on the bank of the Macal River in Belize. My question to Lucy ("So, what are you planning for 2012?") ended up being quite a fertile seed. Thank you.

My next *agradecimientos* go to Edwin Barnhart, Robert Sitler, Mark Van Stone, John Major Jenkins, and James Reed, who helped sort things out for me. I appreciate your time, gentlemen. And to the rest of my interviewees, *muchas gracias también*: Allan Moore, Aluna Joy Yaxk'in, Gaspar Pedro González, Barbara MacLeod, Alfonso Muralles, Dawn Engler, and Florencio Cali. (Note: If your Q&A does not appear in this book, then we ran out of room and it will be published online.)

Thank you to my fellow Moon authors for advice, text, and collegial support: Al Argueta, author of *Moon Guatemala*; Liza Prado and Gary Chandler, authors of *Moon Yucatán, Moon Cancún & Cozumel,* and *Moon Chiapas*; and Amy Robertson and Chris Humphrey, authors of *Moon Honduras*. Also, photographer Eric Mohl and journalist Karen Catchpole helped me conduct some research in the midst of their open-ended Trans-Americas Journey (follow their slow, epic expedition at www.trans-americas.com).

Thanks to the tourist board contacts, tour operators, and jungle lodge owners who responded to my rushed, time-sensitive queries and contributed to this book by offering interesting things to do in their beautiful countries—in 2012 and beyond.

My neighbors at Nomad helped with everything from physical therapy (I'm grateful, Phil), to emergency babysitting (thank you, Halonah and Leslie!), to celebratory drinks after I clicked "send" (*danke,* Kavika and Angelique). Thank you to my colleagues at Shining Mountain Waldorf School for your encouragement—and to all my students, *mil gracias* for making me get off the computer every day and for singing with me.

My wife and daughters were patient and supportive beyond belief during several remarkably busy months. I promise to take you somewhere special next year.

Finally, to my team at Avalon Travel and Perseus Books, I'm proud to work with all of you. Thanks for all you do.

www.moon.com

DESTINATIONS | ACTIVITIES | BLOGS | MAPS | BOOKS

MOON.COM is ready to help plan your next trip! Filled with fresh trip ideas and strategies, author interviews, informative travel blogs, a detailed map library, and descriptions of all the Moon guidebooks, Moon.com is all you need to get out and explore the world—or even places in your own backyard. While at Moon.com, sign up for our monthly e-newsletter for updates on new releases, travel tips, and expert advice from our on-the-go Moon authors. As always, when you travel with Moon, expect an experience that is uncommon and truly unique.

MAP SYMBOLS

▭ Expressway	◖ Highlight	✈ Airport	⚓ Golf Course
▭ Primary Road	○ City/Town	✕ Airfield	P Parking Area
▭ Secondary Road	◉ State Capital	▲ Mountain	⬟ Archaeological Site
▭ Unpaved Road	⊛ National Capital	✛ Unique Natural Feature	⬤ Church
▭ Trail	★ Point of Interest	⌇ Waterfall	⛽ Gas Station
▭ Ferry	• Accommodation	⚲ Park	Glacier
▭ Railroad	▼ Restaurant/Bar	⛺ Trailhead	Mangrove
▭ Pedestrian Walkway	■ Other Location		Reef
▭ Stairs	⋀ Campground	⛷ Skiing Area	Swamp

CONVERSION TABLES

°C = (°F − 32) / 1.8
°F = (°C x 1.8) + 32
1 inch = 2.54 centimeters (cm)
1 foot = 0.304 meters (m)
1 yard = 0.914 meters
1 mile = 1.6093 kilometers (km)
1 km = 0.6214 miles
1 fathom = 1.8288 m
1 chain = 20.1168 m
1 furlong = 201.168 m
1 acre = 0.4047 hectares
1 sq km = 100 hectares
1 sq mile = 2.59 square km
1 ounce = 28.35 grams
1 pound = 0.4536 kilograms
1 short ton = 0.90718 metric ton
1 short ton = 2,000 pounds
1 long ton = 1.016 metric tons
1 long ton = 2,240 pounds
1 metric ton = 1,000 kilograms
1 quart = 0.94635 liters
1 US gallon = 3.7854 liters
1 Imperial gallon = 4.5459 liters
1 nautical mile = 1.852 km

°FAHRENHEIT °CELSIUS
230 — 110
220
210 — 100 WATER BOILS
200
190 — 90
180 — 80
170
160 — 70
150
140 — 60
130
120 — 50
110
100 — 40
90 — 30
80
70 — 20
60
50 — 10
40
30 — 0 WATER FREEZES
20
10 — -10
0
-10 — -20
-20 — -30
-30
-40 — -40

Clock face: 12(24), 1(13), 2(14), 3(15), 4(16), 5(17), 6(18), 7(19), 8(20), 9(21), 10(22), 11(23)

INCH 0 1 2 3 4

CM 0 1 2 3 4 5 6 7 8 9 10

MOON MAYA 2012
Avalon Travel
a member of the Perseus Books Group
1700 Fourth Street
Berkeley, CA 94710, USA
www.moon.com

Editor: Sabrina Young
Copy Editor: Amy Scott
Production and Graphics Coordinator: Tabitha Lahr
Cover Designer: Tabitha Lahr
Map Editor: Mike Morgenfeld

ISBN-13: 978-1-61238-119-0

Printing History
1st Edition – September 2011
5 4 3 2 1

Text © 2011 by Joshua Berman.
The following text is used with permission and is the property of the original copyright holders:
© Liza Prado and Gary Chandler, authors of *Moon Cancún & Cozumel*, *Moon Yucatán Peninsula* and *Moon Chiapas*.
© Al Argueta, author of *Moon Guatemala*.
© Chris Humphrey and Amy E. Robertson, authors of *Moon Honduras & the Bay Islands*.

Maps © 2011 by Avalon Travel.
All rights reserved.

Some photos and illustrations are used by permission and are the property of the original copyright owners.

Front cover photo: © 2011 Tony Rath Photography/ www.tonyrath.com

Title page photo: Temple at Lamanai, Belize © Joshua Berman
Frontmatter photos: Page 3, carvings at Copán © Amy E. Robertson; Page 4 (icon) 'Old Man' at the Acropolis © Amy E. Robertson; Page 4 (bottom), Frieze reconstruction in Maya Hill (Cerros) in northern Belize © Joshua Berman; Page 5 (top left), traditional medicine using flowers and herbs © Joshua Berman; Page 5 (top right), Mundo Maya celebration © Joshua Berman; Page 5 (bottom left), orchid in Mexico © Joshua Berman; Page 5 (bottom right), Owl dancer at Xcaret © Joshua Berman; Pages 6-16 © Joshua Berman

Printed in Canada by Friesens

KEEPING CURRENT

If you have a favorite gem you'd like to see included in the next edition, or see anything that needs updating, clarification, or correction, please drop us a line. Send your comments via email to feedback@moon.com, or use the address above.

ABOUT THE AUTHOR

Joshua Berman

Joshua Berman has been traveling, living, teaching, and leading trips in Central America since 1998, the year the Peace Corps sent him to Nicaragua as an education volunteer. During his two and a half years there, he heard tales about "lost worlds" and Maya pyramids somewhere up the isthmus, and eventually worked his way north, stopping along the way to dive in Honduras and write a guidebook to Belize. He has taken students to Guatemala and El Salvador, guided film crews into caves in Belize, and shared some truly bizarre foods with Travel Channel host Andrew Zimmern.

Joshua is a freelance writer, Spanish teacher, and television production fixer who bounces between Colorado and Latin America. He is a proud alumnus of Brown University, AmeriCorps, Outward Bound, and the Whiskeytown Fire Use Module. In addition to *Moon Maya 2012*, Joshua is the author of *Moon Belize* and the coauthor of *Moon Nicaragua* and *Moon Living Abroad in Nicaragua*. His work has appeared in *The New York Times, Yoga Journal, Outside Traveler, 5280, Sunset, National Geographic Traveler, The Boston Globe, Worldview,* and *Mountain Gazette.* He hopes 2012 will be a year of continuing discovery for himself and his family.

Joshua's Twitter handle is @TranquiloTravel and his home page is www.JoshuaBerman.net.